The Scorecard

THE

Scorecard

· · · · ·

How to Fix Your Man in
One Year or Less

· · · · ·

JULIE BELL

AND

DONNA BROWN

WITH JUDITH NEWMAN

GOTHAM BOOKS

GOTHAM BOOKS
Published by Penguin Group (USA) Inc.
375 Hudson Street, New York, New York 10014, U.S.A. Penguin Group (Canada),
90 Eglinton Avenue East, Suite 700, Toronto, Ontario M4P 2Y3, Canada (a division
of Pearson Penguin Canada Inc.); Penguin Books Ltd, 80 Strand, London
WC2R 0RL, England; Penguin Ireland, 25 St Stephen's Green, Dublin 2, Ireland
(a division of Penguin Books Ltd); Penguin Group (Australia), 250 Camberwell
Road, Camberwell, Victoria 3124, Australia (a division of Pearson Australia Group
Pty Ltd); Penguin Books India Pvt Ltd, 11 Community Centre, Panchsheel Park,
New Delhi – 110 017, India; Penguin Group (NZ), cnr Airborne and Rosedale Roads,
Albany, Auckland 1310, New Zealand (a division of Pearson New Zealand Ltd);
Penguin Books (South Africa) (Pty) Ltd, 24 Sturdee Avenue, Rosebank,
Johannesburg 2196, South Africa

Penguin Books Ltd, Registered Offices: 80 Strand, London WC2R 0RL, England

Published by Gotham Books, a division of Penguin Group (USA) Inc.

First printing, May 2006
10   9   8   7   6   5   4   3   2   1

Gotham Books and the skyscraper logo are trademarks of Penguin Group (USA) Inc.

LIBRARY OF CONGRESS CATALOGING-IN-PUBLICATION DATA
Brown, Donna, 1963–
    The scorecard : how to fix your man in one year or less / Donna Brown and Julie
Bell ; with Judith Newman.
       p.   cm.
    ISBN 1-59240-201-1
1. Man-woman relationships. 2. Interpersonal relations. 3. Interpersonal
communication. I. Bell, Julie, 1973– II. Newman, Judith. III. Title.
    HQ801.B862 2006
    646.7'8—dc22   2005033187

Printed in the United States of America
Set in Filosofia
Designed by Mia Risberg

To Dave, who is proof that heroes exist, people can change, and a man with a mission can overcome all obstacles. All the muches, db

To Phillip, my husband and my hero. Thank you for rescuing me from a life without you—twice. I adore you and I love the bricks. Eli's coming! JBV

Thanks to my men, large and small: John, Augustus, and Henry. JN

. . . and to j—xoxo—db and JBV

Contents

....

We know what we are, but know not what we may be.
—William Shakespeare, *Hamlet*, act 4, scene 5

The Scorecard

Introduction

....

> There is nothing more difficult to take in hand,
> more perilous to conduct, or more uncertain in its
> success, than to take the lead in the introduction of a
> new order of things.
>
> —NICCOLÒ MACHIAVELLI
> *The Prince* (1532)

Which of these gifts from your husband says "I love you" most passionately?

A. Flowers
B. Chocolates
C. Diamonds
D. Windshield-wiper fluid

If you answered anything but "D," you obviously don't live in the Midwest, and you've never been through one of our winters. Julie's story is a perfect example:

There are few seasons more grim than winter in Chicago. Days of icy wind and gray sludge grind down the soul—and wreak havoc on your windshield. From 2000 to late 2002—the darkest years of her marriage—if Julie had asked her husband to do something as simple as make sure she had windshield-wiper fluid, she could guarantee it wouldn't be there.

That's why she cursed herself on a Monday evening in October 2002. The drive from her office at United Airlines near O'Hare Airport to her home in the Chicago suburb of Woodridge takes an hour during rush hour. It's only twenty miles. But in midwinter, with all the cars splashing one another with slush and gunk, you can go through a gallon of windshield-wiper fluid quickly. This fluid is as essential as gasoline. That's what Julie was thinking as she entered the house: I'm out of wiper fluid and the ride to work tomorrow is going to be hell.

"Dang," she fumed to her husband, Phillip, a Chicago city policeman, as she kissed him hello and prepared to help their ten-year-old daughter, Lauren, with her homework, "I'm out of wiper fluid again."

The next morning, Julie fired up her Ford Escape to take Lauren to school. Automatically, she pressed the wiper button to clear the windshield. She didn't know what she was expecting. She knew the container under the hood was empty. Yet there it was: a powerful stream of fluid, clearing her vision. Sometime in the middle of the night, in the bitter cold, Phillip must have bought fluid, then gone out to the driveway and refilled her Escape. She looked in the rearview mirror to catch Lauren's eye as she was reading Harry Potter. *"I love your father," Julie said.*

Pleased but puzzled, Lauren asked, "Why, what did he do? Give you a gift?"

"No, it's better than that. There's wiper fluid in my car!"

Lauren just rolled her eyes and went back to her book. Julie thought, Someday you'll understand. Sex and flowers and jewelry are all very well—but windshield-wiper fluid is sublime. Because it meant the return of the man she had married. He'd remembered what she needed. Which meant he loved her.

Do you ever ask yourself, *What happened to the guy I fell in love with?* Is he still in there somewhere, hidden behind the beer-stained sweat suit and three-day stubble? Is the guy who can't get off the couch the one who made passionate love to me, standing up against the adobe wall in Santa Fe? When was the last time we had a discussion about politics, movies, books . . . or about anything, for that matter, that didn't involve the children or the IRS?

There are very few wives who wouldn't tweak their partners here or there, given the opportunity. But as we all know, getting a man to change is about as likely as getting Cruella de Ville to join PETA. You can nag your husband, plead with him, charm, bribe, coddle, or simply scream like a harpy year after year—and find that nothing makes any difference. No matter what you do, most men won't budge. In fact, most *people* won't budge. When we think about how very difficult it is for a person to evolve, we think about that observation by the British statesman Oliver Cromwell: "He who stops being better stops being good."

Husbands can become fabulously adept at tuning us out. There is a *Far Side* cartoon that always reminds us of our marriages. It has two panels. The first is called "What We Say to Dogs," showing a man shouting at his dog, Ginger: "Okay, Ginger! I've had it! You stay out of the garbage! Understand,

Ginger? Stay out of the garbage, or else!" The second panel is titled: "What Dogs Hear," showing the dog listening while the man says, "blah blah GINGER blah blah blah blah blah GINGER blah blah blah."

And there, in a nutshell, is the marriage of half the women in America.

Women are the primary breadwinners in more than a third of all American families, and yet year after year studies consistently show that working wives are still responsible for the majority of domestic and child-rearing tasks. Forget the old stereotype of the older man leaving his wife for a younger woman. The *real* truth of midlife divorce, according to one large government-funded study conducted by psychologist Sanford Braver at Arizona State University, is that among couples over forty it is women who instigate divorce two-thirds of the time.

As wives will tell you, most men simply don't do their share of the work necessary in raising children and maintaining a viable household. That was certainly the case in our homes. Pushed beyond our limits, we finally responded with our own version of the rallying cry from the classic movie *Network*—"I'm mad as hell and I'm not going to take it anymore!"

If you've ever felt that same white-hot fury, this is the perfect book for you.

How can you get your partner to change? Or, more precisely, how can you get him to change *back* to the person you fell in love with? Our answer to that virtually universal question is *The Scorecard*, a revolutionary new tool we developed for our own husbands. Determined to save our marriages, we succeeded beyond our wildest dreams—and you can, too.

This book was written to provide every woman with the strategy, support, and encouragement to identify what she deserves—and to insist on getting it. A blueprint for change that can radically improve any relationship, *The Scorecard* is really a checklist of requirements for a modern marriage—a women's declaration of independence and bill of rights, rolled into one.

But like any revolution, this one was born out of profound dissatisfaction and turmoil.

If you had met either of us a few years ago, you would never have guessed we were about as happy in our relationships as Woody Allen and Mia Farrow, Ike and Tina Turner, Othello and . . . well, you get the idea. On the surface, you would think our lives were in terrific shape. At the time we each had two healthy children, lovely homes, and dynamic careers that were advancing rapidly. We both lived near Chicago and worked for the same company. We even knew each other.

But neither of us knew the desperate reality behind the other's shiny, happy facade. We always assumed *we* were the only ones tortured by our husbands, and everyone else was married to Tom Hanks.

By 2001, each of us had arrived at a painful turning point in our lives. Both our husbands were unhappy in their work and taking their frustrations out on us. Both seemed to be stalled in chronic midlife crises that left them directionless and depressed. Neither was doing enough to share the burdens of running a household. Both had withdrawn from participating in family life, becoming alienated from their children as well as from their wives. Our men ricocheted daily between being party boys and penitents, and were generally in such perpetual crisis they were making everyone around them miserable. And we had turned into women who were so focused on holding it all together that our lives had become about logistics rather than joy.

We felt trapped by the social paradigm of our time, where

women are expected to "have it all," blissfully happy and balanced, with no mention of painful tradeoffs and identity crises. Trapped by knowing that our husbands were good and loving men who just needed a chance to get it together. Trapped by not wanting to admit defeat.

After years of trying to get them to shape up, we had finally given up. Nothing had worked: No amount of begging, fighting, or pleading had helped our partners put their lives or our marriages back on track.

At this point each of us independently arrived at the same conclusion: We were not willing to go forward with unresponsive husbands who refused to address our concerns or shoulder their own responsibilities (let alone ours).

So we did the one thing we never thought we'd have the strength to do: We kicked them out.

We had lost all hope of fixing our miserable marriages, and we were ready to start new lives. We were so anxious to get rid of our spouses that we even helped them pack. Which is no great surprise. It was second nature for us to clean up their messes; at this point we couldn't even depend on them to know how to get dumped without our help.

Please don't think either of us took such a momentous step lightly. On television it looks so easy: *Kick him to the curb!*, women cry on *Montel* and *Maury* and *Jerry Springer*. Real women—and real mothers—know just how agonizing it is. It's daunting enough to become a single parent when you have no control over what's happening. But we were proactively choosing that course, with all the guilt it entailed.

Ironically, it was our optimism that held us back. Because we are by nature hopeful people, each disappointment felt a little bigger than the last. We were forever looking for signs our husbands would get better—that *we* would get better—and they never came. Or worse, our men would promise to change and the results wouldn't be there. We both saw moments that reminded us of our great pasts together. There was a time when our lives were about family and being together, and everything else—the taxes, the endless logistics of having small children, the errands—was all background noise. But the background noise had become so deafeningly loud, it was like living in an airplane hangar. We could not hear each other, we could not connect, over that terrible racket.

We realized only too well that our children would be hurt in the process. We knew they would feel confused and upset about what was happening. We understood that they would miss their fathers, no matter how much their dads had disappointed them.

But we also knew that our children's identities were being shaped by fathers who were unmotivated and emotionally unavailable. We no longer trusted Phillip and Dave to be reliable guardians of their kids' welfare while we were at work. We didn't feel we could count on our partners for the most basic tasks, let alone for the kind of stimulation, support, and joy we had expected to find in marriage.

After a great deal of soul-searching, we both came to the same conclusion: No matter what hardships a separation might bring, the end result would be worth it if we were able to create a happier future for all of us, whether together or apart.

Although it does share a certain spirit of "tough love," *The Scorecard* isn't *The Rules* for marriage. The decision to separate, and the list of tasks our husbands had to perform before we'd get back together, wasn't a strategy to manipulate our mates. We were fed up with our partners and their broken promises, their failures to communicate, their bottomless unhappiness, their inertia. They had let us down in so many ways that we didn't even love them anymore—or so we thought.

Frankly, we couldn't have been more shocked by what happened next. Miracles do happen—and this is the story of two such miracles.

Why do you have to practically thump a man with a two-by-four to get his attention? We haven't figured that one out yet. What we did figure out, however, was the kind of relationships we deserved.

And, we should add, the kind of relationships *they* deserved. Because as our marriages unraveled, we weren't exactly the most delightful people to live with, either. The nagging and screaming had become a vicious cycle: We were stuck in the role of Nagging Mom and our husbands had been cast as the Bitter, Sullen Teenagers.

But that, you see, is the miracle of doing *The Scorecard* (and, in fact, the big idea buried in our book): *If one person in a marriage is transformed, so is his mate.* Our husbands' metamorphosis was also our own.

What is required for this, or indeed *any*, transformation? An entirely new approach, one that comes naturally to most women in the workplace but not at home. We will explain more thoroughly in the next chapter on "How to Use *The Scorecard*," but essentially it comes down to this: You must step back from your relationship and, to the best of your ability, look at it as you might a business problem.

✳ About *The Scorecard* ✳

The Scorecard's origins are rooted in our business experience. At various times in our lives we've pondered the same question as millions of women have: How can we be so effective at work and so ineffective in our own homes?

Then we had an epiphany.

Any successful executive, when confronted with a professional challenge, knows what to do. You determine a desired outcome. You set the goals required to reach it. You pick the winning team, and you delegate responsibility to that team, making them responsible for achieving those goals.

In many corporate environments, the paradigm is the so-called Balanced Scorecard—a performance management tool used to track and measure the health of a business. Here's how it works: In the workplace there are often many ways to look at the same project. You can define a project in a positive light (it will be completed on time, for example) or you can choose a negative perspective (that is, we had to spend twice as much money to keep it on track). The Balanced Scorecard approach selects the most important parameters to any project and measures them consistently over time. One project, as an example, may have the following parameters established: a) *Spending* (How much are we spending on this project compared to our budget?); b) *Timeline* (Is the project going to be delivered on time? Which tasks are off track, and which ones have been completed?); c) *Resources* (How many people do we have allocated to this project?), etc. A Scorecard enables a project manager to see all the issues before him/her without hiding anything. With a Scorecard, if some aspect of the work goes off track, the problem can be addressed as quickly as possible to ensure the project's ultimate success.

Donna spent fifteen years in the human resources field, with such great brands as United Airlines, Ernst & Young, and General Electric. Many have said, what you don't learn about HR at GE isn't worth knowing—and this is largely true. HR is, on the most fundamental level, about optimizing every element of the work process—the workplace, the performance of each employee, team performance, and ultimately the performance of the company. Because every situation is different, HR specialists are perpetually assessing the tactics to use for a given challenge, monitoring progress, and calibrating the results.

Julie is a strategic sourcing director at United Airlines as it works its way through one of the more painful bankruptcies of recent years. She is a tough negotiator, scrapping for every penny of savings with suppliers and vendors. To Julie, the marriage contract is not so different from a company's contract with any service provider or supplier. Once a contract is signed, the company pays close attention to the supplier's performance, taking corrective action if the supplier fails to meet any of its contractual obligations.

These were the skill sets we brought to our domestic woes. We knew how to assess performance, how to correct it, and how to measure the results of corrective action. So we took what we knew worked in business and applied it at home. We each created a Scorecard for our husbands to improve both themselves and our marriage—just as if we were implementing a model for problem solving in the workplace. We did it first by identifying the areas that needed improvement and defining our expectations, and then by giving our partners specific tasks and determining the necessary measurements to hold them accountable for improvement. It may sound cold and rigorous and corporate, but it was all we had to fall back on.

And it worked.

✳ Your Marriage, Your Scorecard ✳

The stories detailed here may be particular to us, but the overall story of our marriages is not. Far from it. And the truth is: When it comes to marriage, we all have different deal breakers. For one wife, it might be the Other Woman; for another, it might be a husband who gambles away the paycheck or who keeps his children at arm's distance. And many more of you have marital problems that are much less serious yet are seriously impeding your ability to enjoy family life. (OK, so you may not want to divorce your husband because he's out four nights a week at karaoke bars and has decided to audition for *American Idol*. But really, you think to yourself: Do I *have* to put up with this?)

Whatever your gripe (or gripes), there are some parts of *The Scorecard* that apply to you.

Our marriages took approximately a year to fix (hence our book title). Most marriages, with far less serious problems, will take less time; some will take considerably more. And we freely admit that some marriages—where there is violence, profound neglect, compulsive cheating—perhaps can't and *shouldn't* be fixed. But we believe you're reading this book because your memories of the "good old days" with your mate are still strong—and you feel confident you can recapture them. We're here to help you do just that.

✳ Changing the Course of Our Marriages ✳
—and Our Lives

The prerequisites we set for reconciliation were tough and un-compromising, though our tactics for getting our husbands' compliance were slightly different. Julie actually presented her husband with a list of tasks he had to complete (slightly less detailed than the one we've devised here) if he wanted to stay married. Julie knew this list was too much to ask. Phillip ended up proving her wrong. Donna had a remarkably similar list, which she kept to herself, revealing her requests in conversations and making her "list" known in what she hoped was a logical, orderly, and manageable fashion. At the time, Donna's list was more of an itemization of things Dave should do to have more joy in his life. It wasn't necessarily a list for fixing a marriage. But sometimes life works out *better* than you planned it.

Some of the items on the checklist required our husbands to develop a greater sense of self-respect. Some required them to show more respect to their wives. Still others involved the respect they accorded the family.

Both of us assumed our partners would be unable to satisfy our conditions. We were astonished as our husbands rose to the Herculean challenges we had set for them. They changed themselves, their attitudes toward us, and their behavior within the family. They changed their habits and modified their expectations.

And we changed, too.

Both of us had, at some point in our lives, what I now think of as the Tammy Wynette, Stand-by-Your-Man philosophy of marriage. We would stand by our men, no matter what. Isn't

this what marriage was all about? (Of course, people don't remember the thrice-married Wynette's less popular tunes, "I
Don't Want to Play House" and "D-I-V-O-R-C-E.")

And both of us equated love with mind reading: *If you love
me, you'll suddenly become the Amazing Kreskin, anticipating my
needs and desires at every turn.*

Well, things don't work that way—and things particularly don't
work that way with men. You've got to remove the guesswork.

After a one-year separation, both of us got back together
with our mates . . . and each of us is now happier than we have
ever been or believed we could be. And with our husbands'
transformations, we found out that *we've* become more loving,
sensual women.

But the biggest surprise came when we compared notes. Although we are very different people, each of us, unbeknownst to
the other, had arrived at almost the same checklist for a healthy
relationship. True, there were certain specifics that weren't
relevant to the other's marriage—one of us had a husband who
partied too much; one had a problem with depression. But
when we looked at our lists, we discovered that while there were
subtle differences, there were essentially nine areas of improvement we had both demanded of our mates. These nine areas became the backbone of *The Scorecard*:

- Communicate: Become My Friend
- Deal: Become Self-sufficient
- Work: Become Productive
- Love: Become an Involved Father
- Celebrate: Become a Believer in Ritual
- Play: Become My Lover
- Share: Become a Domestic God

- Plan: Become Fiscally Responsible
- Evolve: Become the Man You Want to Be

We All Want Our Men to Start Talking and Keep Talking: It's not like we're asking men to learn English as a second language . . . but it's close. A breakdown in communication is often the first major problem in a marriage. We need to know what our guys think . . . about us, about our lives together, about what's going on in their heads and hearts. More than anything, we want our guys to talk as bluntly and honestly to us as they do to the talking heads on ESPN.

We All Want Our Men to Be Self-sufficient. By *self-sufficient*, we don't mean simply, "Bring home the bucks." We are talking about the inability of many men to deal with the niggling details of life, the ones that so many men avoid—even if *they're* the stay-at-homes and *we're* the ones working. "I don't know how" is no excuse. Learn.

We All Want Our Men to Be Productive: Again, this is not necessarily a question of how much a man earns. It is a question of finding something he's passionate about and doing it. Fact is, when a man is happy and passionate about what he does, he tends to bring those positive emotions home to his wife and family.

This step is one of the hardest, because the challenge was not just for our husbands but for us. We had to let go of *our* definition of the Perfect Husband before we could support our spouse's success. Letting go isn't easy after you've controlled (or tried to control) everything for so long.

We All Want Our Men to Be Fathers to Their Children: We have a friend, still married, who often refers to her husband as "the sperm donor." It's a reflection of how involved she thinks he is in their lives. We suspect she won't be married for long. (Unless of course, she heeds the advice in this book!)

We all want our men to be *active* fathers. This doesn't mean he has to teach them to rock climb or hunt grizzlies. It does mean he has to be there to support and encourage his children's pursuits—pursuits that go beyond watching *SpongeBob Square-Pants* and playing *Doom*.

We All Want Our Men to Help Us Create a Feeling of Family: The dad who's donning the Santa suit or assembling the tricycle or just making sure the wee ones buy us flowers for Mother's Day . . . those contributions, where he helps celebrate holidays and the passing of the seasons (as compared to uttering those popular husbandly words, "Oh, well, I just forgot") make us feel like a family instead of a group of people who share a house and some DNA.

We All Want Our Men to Know What We Find Hot: Let's face it: Monogamy is kind of weird. When the idea of sleeping with one person forever came into vogue, it was probably at a time when everyone died at forty-five; "forever" wasn't that long a time. So now . . . if we're only allowed to sleep with one person, it had better be good.

Did you ever hear the saying, "Men use love to get sex; women use sex to get love"? As long as everyone is getting love *and* having sex, this works. If the bargain falls apart, it doesn't. Besides, wouldn't it be easier for women to maintain just one sex life instead of two (the one with their husbands and the one with themselves)?

We All Want Our Men to Know How to Chop Onions and Accurately Measure One Cup of Laundry Detergent: Really, we don't expect much. He doesn't have to be able to cook; if he can be the chopper/sous-chef, that's great. If he can't fold, at least let him know that the new neon-blue sweater doesn't go in with the whites. He doesn't have to be Martha Stewart (because God knows we aren't), but he can't be dumb as lint about domestic niceties, either.

We All Want Our Men to Contribute to Our Family's Financial Well-Being: Whether it's a paycheck or some other form of contribution, men need to contribute to their way of life. We are all for stay-at-home dads (SAHDs)—hey, at one time we both thought it a great way to balance our financial and family needs. The problem is, we have lived with the SAHDs, and bitter experience has taught us that most men (not all, but most) are not equipped to take on this role. So while the spirit may be willing, the flesh (and there will be lots more of it, once they are five steps away from the refrigerator all day) is weak. They don't have to bring home paychecks bigger than or equal to ours. But they do have to pour a few pesos into the pot. Especially since some form of paycheck seems to be inextricably tied to their feelings of self-worth.

Being financially responsible is part of looking toward the future with someone. Indeed, Aesop's fable about the grasshopper and the ant is true for too many of us. We hope that the person we build a life with thinks about the foundation of that edifice. Celebrating today is wonderful if you know there's a little something left over for tomorrow.

We All Want Our Men to Become the Best They Can Be: We have always appreciated the observation of Sam Walton, founder of Wal-Mart, about being a good manager: "Outstanding leaders go out of their way to boost the self-esteem of their personnel. If people believe in themselves, it's amazing what they can accomplish." And we do believe that if it's true for a business, it's also true for a marriage: You have to be your husband's champion. But in our personal lives, women have a tendency to take this idea too far. One of our most common fantasies is this: *I am so wonderful, and have so much to offer, that my presence in your life will make you happy.* Um, no.

Without exactly setting out to do it, we think we have created a man/woman bill of rights with this list. In that sense, our Scorecards became an instruction manual for change, in order to pursue happiness and achieve those inalienable rights.

Any successful business model requires you to assess where you are in the present and figure out where you want to go in the future. That's what we did with our marriages—quantifying the goals so precisely there could be no argument or ambiguity about whether they had been accomplished. In devising our Scorecards, we inadvertently created a powerful tool that can help anyone, no matter what her circumstance.

This is a story about women's empowerment—about how far women have come in the last couple of generations, and how different their lives can be as a result. In earlier eras, women put up with their husbands no matter what they did, because divorce was stigmatized and wives were almost always financially dependent. Men could be deadbeats, philanderers, abusers, drunkards, and drug addicts—and still their wives stayed with them, unable to envision an independent life without their husbands' support.

Those days are gone.

And this is, in the end, a book about change: why it is necessary and how to accomplish it. An inspirational story about the power of love, *The Scorecard* provides a potent illustration of every individual's ability to change, in the most fundamental and difficult ways, and to recreate themselves when they finally realize they will lose everything they care about. This is why our husbands, Dave and Phillip, are the ultimate heroes of this saga. Faced with the disintegration of their families, these men simply refused to accept defeat. They were determined to make whatever changes were necessary to save their marriages. Both of them succeeded beyond our wildest dreams, winning back our respect, earning our devotion, and turning failure into triumph.

A Little Background
on *The Scorecard—*
and Us

· · · · ·

Donna was twenty-six when she first met Dave in San Diego. Ostensibly, she worked as an office manager, but her real job was perfecting her tan. Career? What was that? There was a beach to hit and parties to go to. . . . Let's just say that youth was not wasted.

While all of this was fun, and dating a big part of it, Donna specialized in romances that seemed mostly out of balance and more in line with midday soap operas than fodder for a lasting relationship. She enjoyed the drama, but drama wears thin. She didn't want to spend every waking moment worrying about being enchanting; mostly, she wanted a relationship where she could be herself.

Enter Dave. Rescued by her friends from pining away after a relationship gone wrong, Donna met Dave while on a dancing spree in Tijuana. She fell in love with him on the way to the Iguana Club, to be precise (there's a song in there somewhere).

He was twenty-three, a navy man, dark-eyed, dark-haired, and a big teddy bear. Everyone loved Dave: He was attentive, charming, a bit shy, and when she started to cross the street on a busy Saturday night in TJ—where "traffic light" and "stop," even in Spanish, get lost in translation—he gently took her hand in protection. That was the moment Donna knew: He was her knight in shining armor.

And, in a sense, Donna was not far from wrong. Donna knew she was a tad high-strung and high-maintenance, whereas Dave had what she called living-room magnetism: He was naturally at ease with people. He was a romantic who remembered birthdays, anniversaries, and everything about their first date.

Donna and Dave came from opposite ends of the socioeconomic spectrum—which at first made everything more exciting. She came from affluent Greenwich, Connecticut, where her father was the big-time breadwinner and center of the family. Dave came from a poor family in Michigan that didn't have a phone until he went away to the navy and a stepfather who believed strongly in corporal punishment. Donna and her friends shared a cosmopolitan lifestyle, and had began planning college and travel experiences in junior high. Most of Dave's friends became parents, married or not, before they hit twenty. Donna's life was an escape; Dave joined the navy to escape to a better life.

So, when Donna met Dave, his determination to make something more of his life and experience new things was particularly touching to her. Also touching: Dave's quietly stated desire to be an involved, loving father.

Dave and Donna married in 1992 and had their son, Philip, the following year. And, like so many women, Donna knew that being pregnant meant she'd have to put some of the past behind her. No more booze, cigarettes, and partying. With little warning, Dave lost his good-time girl. What he had instead was a woman thinking about her family and her career . . . about money, about the future. Suddenly, things that never occurred to them before—*What about life insurance?*—were front and center in Donna's mind.

A second child, Chelsea, followed almost five years later. Dave was a wonderful father to both children—getting up in the middle of the night, sharing diaper duty, teaching the kids all of the things that fathers want to teach their children—which is what Donna had known he would be. The fact that he was not at all career ambitious allowed him to work a forty-hour week and be done so he could spend time with the family, which is what Donna wanted. She didn't care what he did, as long as he was happy and that whatever he did allowed him to be present and engaged in the family they were building.

While all this was happening, however, Donna began to focus and realize her own career ambitions. While she had struggled after college to decide what she really wanted to do (law school was nixed after an internship in a corporate law practice, teaching Victorian literature was nixed after she realized that being a successful teacher involves publishing—fancy that—and is strangely political), her first full-time corporate job at GE Capital showed her her destiny: a career in human resources; it fit her like a glove. As she began to move up the corporate ladder, Dave was happy to move from job to job: managing a warehouse, selling spiral staircases, being a pastry chef. At first, this seemed like a good balance for them (no way were they going to become an urban power couple). Unfortunately, however, their paths began to diverge and—though they didn't know it at the time—this, along with the choices they would make, would take them from a happy family to a family at the point of disintegration.

Donna and Dave had moved to Connecticut to start their married lives. Living in the tristate area is financially brutal, and Greenwich—where Donna and Dave lived—has some of the most expensive real estate in the nation. Wanting to gain a better balance, Dave began talking about returning to the Midwest. Well, no way was Donna moving to Michigan, but Chicago . . . well, if a terrific job landed on her lap, the pay was right, and they came and packed her house, loaded up her cars, and put her on a plane . . . maybe . . . And, as life happens, nine months later they were in the Windy City. After long discussions about the fact that they did not want to both be working full-time when their children were young, they finally had the chance to make their dream a reality: Dave could stay home with the kids and manage the household while Donna went off to her new job with an office in the Sears Tower. Fully understanding the difficulties that stay-at-home dads face, they didn't plan a time frame—even a few months would be a benefit to their children, Philip, who had just entered kindergarten, and Chelsea, who was a few months old.

At first, everything was wonderful, and they were thrilled to have such an important opportunity. Donna loved her new job and Dave and the children seemed to be thriving. Dave settled seamlessly into his new role and even experienced the added benefit of a wonderful new physique due to constantly being out with the kids, bike riding, fishing, and generally in "expedition mode." The house was clean, dinner was made. It was June and Ward Cleaver with a bit of a twist.

Over time, however, all of the things that historically have plagued housewives began to plague Dave: He began feeling unfulfilled and unappreciated, and lost his sense of self. With everything at home now someone else's responsibility, Donna began working longer and longer hours at a more and more demanding job as she jockeyed for her next role. Things deteriorated quickly from there.

Suddenly, the housework wasn't done, the kids weren't eating properly, and Dave stopped paying any attention to the logistics of their school, their homework, and their extracurriculars. Far from finding herself free to concentrate on bringing home the bacon, Donna discovered that she had TWO jobs: her's and Dave's.

Donna saw that Dave was depressed, and she tried to talk to him about it. Dave, however, was not equipped to acknowledge depression, never mind discuss it with her. So, she tried to remove responsibilities to make it easier for him; she knew the demands of being a homemaker and admired Dave for lasting so long, but realized that it was time to make a change. Dave, though, didn't seem to be able to transition so quickly, and—if anything—her "assistance" intensified his sense of being useless, which made him more depressed and more disconnected from family and friends.

They became more and more polarized—particularly around their intimate life. As Donna got angrier, her desire to be intimate waned. And, since Dave was someone who measured the health of his marriage by the level of intimacy, he believed their marriage was getting shakier because of the lack of intimacy. But not only was Donna angry because he wasn't pulling his weight, she wasn't even feeling particularly attracted to him because they weren't connecting on an intellectual or emotional level: He was slouching around in sweats and a T-shirt like Michael Keaton in *Mr. Mom*. He wasn't reading anything. He wasn't *doing* anything. Donna began to feel that sharing her life with him was simply a matter of getting through the day.

Donna describes the final straw: "One night, after Dave had come home from playing darts, I awoke at about 3:00 AM to find him not in the house. After a panicky moment, a slow dread crept over me that he was probably out at the bowling alley bar. What to do? Could I have possibly stooped to the level of calling a bar in the middle of the night asking for my husband? Wasn't that a *Roseanne* sitcom? The ultimate humiliation: This is not the kind of life I lead! But, what if something horrible happened? If I don't call and he is lying dead somewhere, I couldn't forgive myself. So I called. I felt so dumb; so stupid. It all fell into place now. This was not my life."

Julie met Phillip when she was twenty-one. Believe it or not, they met when Phillip answered her ad in the personals. At the time, Julie was a single mom living on the beach on Topsail Island, North Carolina, with her roommate. She had moved from her hometown, Wichita, Kansas, when her first husband, Brian, joined the Marine Corps. Being single and living on the beach wasn't bad, but Julie was looking for a better life for her and her daughter, Lauren.

Julie came from a family in which money wasn't abundant and divorce was common. Her own parents divorced when she was only five. Julie's dad was very involved in their lives, but he worked long hours, and her mom worked any overtime she could get at the post office. They did everything they could to give Julie, her sister, and her brother a great life by putting them in Catholic schools and involving them in activities like Tae-Kwon-Do. Eventually, her dad took a job at United Airlines so he could get free travel for the family and start taking vacations.

For Julie, college wasn't a thought until it was impossible, when she found out she was pregnant with Lauren. She got married young, moved to North Carolina, and realized quickly that married life wasn't all fun and that the teenage boy she fell in love with wasn't cut out to be the perfect dad or husband. They were both too young and parted ways. Julie tried the singles' scene, but who wants to talk to a twenty-year-old with a two-year-old daughter? No one. Finally, she heard a motivational speaker say, "If you keep doing what you've always done, expect what you've always had." It all made sense. She got her act together, reenrolled in college classes, and did something that seemed out of character at the time—but worth the risk. She put an ad in the personals. Dozens of calls came in. Boring, too old, too young, not interested in a long-term relationship . . . and finally, she heard the perfect voice. It was Phillip.

She called him back and they talked on the phone for hours. He was the perfect gentleman. It seemed like they had everything in common. He was recently separated as well. She invited him over for dinner. An hour before he arrived, she realized she had three dollars to her name and ran to the grocery store, bought what she could afford—a red bell pepper and some alfredo sauce mix, ran home, threw it on some fettuccine she found in the cabinet, and—*Voila!*—Phillip thought Julie was Julia Child and wouldn't find out for years that it's completely untrue.

Julie was impressed, too. Phillip was polite, incredibly hand-some, and drove a station wagon, which she interpreted as a sign of responsibility and devotion to family. Like Julie, he was in the process of getting a divorce. Phillip was still hurting from the breakup of his marriage. He had hoped to start a family, but his wife had had an affair. He was in pain, and was looking for someone who was settled. Julie had a child; unlike other men who fled the moment they saw Lauren, for Phillp, Lauren and the domesticity she represented was immensely appealing. Be-tween the military man and the three-year-old, it was love at first sight. Phillip came over that first night and pretty much never left. He and Julie did everything together, from running errands to cooking on the grill to holding hands each night walking along the beach. To Julie, Phillip was her knight in shining armor—only instead of riding a steed, he drove up in a station wagon.

In 1996, Julie left North Carolina briefly to go to college in San Francisco, but missed Phillip so much she returned to North Carolina, having been accepted into the University of North Carolina. They were happy. Julie was studying inces-santly; they had a large circle of friends; they shared a love for her daughter; and soon, another little girl was on the way. They had no money—so they grew the tomatoes for the grilled cheese and tomato sandwiches they ate almost daily—but he took fatherhood very seriously, spending time with both his daughters.

Julie hadn't done much planning in her personal life. Every-thing sort of happened to her—love, marriage, babies, divorce. But when she graduated from college at twenty-four, married with two kids, she began to think seriously about her career.

Phillip was getting out of the military. He was a little less motivated about what he wanted to do next, though he thought about becoming a policeman. This goal proved to be trickier than they thought, and while Julie and Phillip waited for him to be accepted into a training program, Julie decided to get her MBA at Rider University in New Jersey. She loved school. And she loved beating the odds of the destiny that had been mapped out for her.

Life seemed to hold so many possibilities.

The only hint of trouble? Phillip was drinking a little more than he used to. And the more he drank, the less focused he became. It's not like he was a bellicose drunk. Quite the contrary: He was very nice and loving. And it was only beer, Julie told herself. But how much was too much?

Julie got her MBA, and in 1999 went to work as a financial analyst for United Airlines in Chicago. The couple moved to a suburb where they didn't know anybody, but they were still happy. Julie was making what she thought was a good salary, and they decided Phillip would stay at home and help the kids get acclimated while he looked for a job.

Big mistake.

He was unmotivated and bored. He drank more. And because he drank more, he became even more unmotivated and bored. Julie, meanwhile, was trying to prove herself in this challenging new job, so she was working until 7:00 or 8:00 every night—barely seeing her husband, let alone her children. While Phillip waited for placement in the Chicago Police Department, he took a tech job, and hated it. Then he took another job, and another. His goal seemed to be drifting farther and farther away.

Phillip began hiding things from Julie—receipts for use-less things he'd bought, empty beer cans. He became in-creasingly introverted and withdrawn; his conversation with his children was sometimes reduced to, "Can you get me a beer?"

It's not that he didn't function; quite the contrary. He made it through the fitness test to become a Chicago Police officer. But he was surly and miserable and uncommunicative. When he didn't drink their intimate life was great. But otherwise every-thing about their home and the kids took a backseat to televi-sion and beer. He still looked great, and the mothers at school fawned over him—which didn't make it easy for Julie, the nag-ging corporate drone who was working sixty hours a week. It was like a middle-American version of *A Star Is Born*: The more Julie achieved, the lower Phillip got.

They screamed at each other constantly. The kids heard it all. It was as if the man she'd married had gone AWOL.

Life was so awful at home that Julie didn't want to come home at all, even to see the kids. Phillip wasn't happy in his job or anywhere else. He knew he wasn't being the best father he could be and he felt guilty about it, but he kept blaming Julie for his drinking and his unhappiness: She wasn't home, which meant she didn't love him. He was drinking, he had a job he hated, and somehow it was all Julie's fault.

It's hard to pinpoint the line you cross when you finally say, "I've had it." Julie had tremendous guilt about asking Phillip to leave; she was full of doubt and self-questioning. Why wasn't she willing to take that step? This question consumed her for days and weeks. Then one day she stared in the mirror and saw a very frightened woman looking back. Julie woke up. She hadn't come this far to be pulled back into the dysfunction she knew all too well from childhood.

We both were facing what looked like an end to the lives we knew. In fact, our lives were only beginning.

Thinking their marriages were beyond repair, Donna and Julie both left their husbands. After getting over the shock of being alone and single parents, they began to take stock of their lives: what they wanted, what they needed, and—most importantly—what they deserved. Enthusiastic listmakers, they began to write down the qualities in a marriage that would enrich their lives. There was pain in being honest; there was also clarity. And so, inadvertently, *The Scorecard* was born.

As with most great ideas, *The Scorecard* was not a *Eureka!* concept; it was more of an evolution. It started as an internal dialogue, and ended up being *the* conversation with their husbands. How? Slowly, their husbands had also been taking stock of their lives. They were out in the cold, and the cold was bitter. They wanted the warmth of their family lives back.

First, Donna and Julie's reaction to their pleas was simple: No way, no how. But their husbands were never ones to take no for an answer. While at first it seemed that little had changed, Dave and Phillip are stubborn, goal-oriented, competitive—and now they had a mission.

At this point Donna and Julie had one whip-smart idea: If their men really wanted to be part of their lives again, they had to meet their list of requirements for a happy relationship. Ah, but the list was long and the men had far to go. Perfect! Because neither Donna nor Julie was certain that reconciling with her spouse was really what she wanted. Being unable to imagine their men meeting the challenges ahead allowed them to leave this question up in limbo. As they each began to communicate their Scorecards to their husbands, their husbands began to accomplish what the women thought was impossible: They began to change. And, as the men began to change, the blossoms of hope for reconciliation began to bloom.

Before You Begin

How to Use The Scorecard

· · · · ·

The fabric of our marriages was so tattered, we still marvel over the fact that we could knit it back together. However, you don't have to be in as bad shape as we were to benefit from this book. We think the old adage "Keep the best and leave the rest" applies here: There will be many readers whose marriages need not an overhaul but a tune-up, and you can flip to the parts of the book that discuss *your* "problem areas." This book is a tool to help you; you don't necessarily need to read from beginning to end.

With the creation and implementation of the Scorecard, we ended up getting what we wanted and needed. Now we want to share what we've learned, which we hope will allow you to apply the same business rigor and common sense to your personal relationships. We are here to tell you that you don't have to be a psychiatrist or a Harvard MBA to do this.

But at the same time, we recognize that fixing a *really* troubled marriage is a lot like dieting. You need to drop five pounds? No problem: Just drink Slim-Fast for a week. You need to drop fifty pounds? Well, it's so overwhelming that instead of putting the time and resources toward dieting, you learn to be complacent about your weight and just buy larger clothes. That's what it was like for us facing what had become truly weighty issues between our husbands and us.

Well, we're here to tell you that, whether your marriage is like having an extra five pounds or an extra fifty, we can help you define a structured approach to getting your marriage in shape. Whether you are in what we like to call Prevention, Correction, or Recovery (that is, whether you want to prevent future problems, correct problems you have today, or recover from the fallout from a bad-but-now-repaired relationship), we know the process of doing the Scorecard will help you enormously.

Often, we felt alone, like *we* were the only ones tortured in our marriages. Not knowing what goes on behind the closed doors of your friends and neighbors keeps you from knowing if you are "normal." Every day we would wonder whether others were having as hard a time as we were deciding where to draw The Line in our relationships. It took us years to discover that the only person who could draw that line was US.

The biggest obstacle to change was to actually tell ourselves—and believe—"I deserve better." It took more courage than we thought to say with confidence that we needed something and to stop worrying about whether or not it was the "right" or "normal" or "fair" thing to need. You can take every *Cosmo* quiz, talk to every girlfriend, and never get the same answer. Your needs don't have to be the universal needs of the entire female gender.

One of the keys to success with the Scorecard is defining for yourself what you want and need out of a relationship. This is not about what you have today or what you had yesterday. And it's not about letting someone else—your mother, your best friend, your shrink—define your needs for you. It's about what *you* want the relationship to be, what *you* want to give to it.

(Pathetic but true: Most of us choose our forever partners based first on chemistry, and everything else is an afterthought. Or, put another way . . . it's safe to say none of us is doing a gap analysis (see below) to see which guy meets most of our needs when we first meet them. So we think most of us NEED to go through this exercise at some point. It would obviously have been most helpful to have done the Scorecard before we chose our spouses—but hey, better late than never.)

If marriage is in one sense a lot like losing weight—easy to change only if the change is minimal—in another, it's a lot like shopping. If you go shopping with a list, you get what was on that list, and generally you are happy at the end of the day. If you shop without the list, you vaguely know there are a ton of things you want, you buy more than you need—and you end up dissatisfied and returning a lot of stuff. Same with marriage: If you're not clear about what you want, you have this vague sense of wanting a lot, and you're always a little critical and dissatisfied with what you have.

Once you've defined what you want, you then need to compare what you want with what you have. In business, this is called a *gap analysis.* We're going to show you a way to conduct this analysis that's simple. (And you can recycle this tool for use in many situations and circumstances.) After you've identified the gaps, you need to figure out your plan of action. This is the part that can be a bit overwhelming, so we have some other tools that will help you sort and prioritize as you go through the process of the Scorecard.

Let's begin:

Start with a clean sheet of paper.
(Or two. Or ten . . .)

STEP ONE: Copy the chart below.

STEP TWO: In the second column, list the items in each category that would make you happy—not items *other* people think are important, necessarily, but rather items that matter to YOU.

STEP THREE: Decide, for each Need and Want, if it is Important (I) or Not Important (N) to you. (We've started you off with our example.)

STEP FOUR: Decide, by category, if you are generally Satisfied (S) with an area or Dissatisfied (D) with an area.

Example: Your chart should look something like this:

CATEGORY	NEEDS AND WANTS	I/N	S/D
COMMUNICATE: Become My Friend	● Talk about what you're thinking and feeling ● Share your opinions and preferences ● Speak your mind in an honest and constructive way ● Open up about what's bothering you ● DON'T YELL!!!!	I	D

CATEGORY	NEEDS AND WANTS	I/N	S/D
	⊕ Keep me apprised of what's going on in your life		
	⊕ Don't make unilateral decisions. Remember that we have a partnership.		
	⊕ Show interest in my work and my life as an individual		
	⊕ Don't take out your anger about other problems on me		
DEAL: **Become** **Self-sufficient**	⊕ Set up your own bank accounts	I	D
	⊕ Balance your own checkbook		
	⊕ Get your own credit cards		
	⊕ Get your own home insurance		
	⊕ Get your own car insurance		
	⊕ Maintain your own car		
	⊕ Furnish your own home		
	⊕ Make your home appropriate and comfortable for children (toys, etc.)		
	⊕ Rent an apartment		
	⊕ Arrange for gas and electricity		
	⊕ Get telephone and cable		
	⊕ Help prepare children for your move		
	⊕ Pack your belongings		
	⊕ Schedule move		
	⊕ Transfer accounts and make change-of-address notifications		
	⊕ Select your own doctors and dentist		

CATEGORY	NEEDS AND WANTS	I/N	S/D
	⊕ Make your own appointments		
	⊕ Follow through with doctors' recommendations		
	⊕ Read and understand your own benefit plans		
	⊕ File your own insurance paperwork		
	⊕ Maximize your benefits and observe compliance requirements		
	⊕ Pay your own bills		
	⊕ Buy your own groceries		
	⊕ Make your own meals		
	⊕ Clean up after yourself		
	⊕ Do your own laundry		
WORK: **Become** **Productive**	⊕ Evaluate your interests	I	S
	⊕ Identify your dream		
	⊕ Pick your career		
	⊕ Develop a plan for working toward career goals		
	⊕ Prepare and send out resume		
	⊕ Reach out to resources (friends, classified ads, employment agencies, etc.)		
	⊕ Study, train, and test for requirements		
	⊕ Obtain necessary certification		
	⊕ Job hunt		

CATEGORY	NEEDS AND WANTS	I/N	S/D
	🌐 Become employed 🌐 Earn enough money to support your desired lifestyle 🌐 Further your progress with long-term career goals		
LOVE: **Become** **an Involved** **Father**	🌐 Talk to your children individually at least once a day 🌐 Keep track of what they're doing, thinking, and feeling 🌐 Play with kids every day 🌐 Read to kids every night 🌐 Take kids to the park 🌐 Go on bike rides with kids 🌐 Go to movies and on other family outings 🌐 Teach each kid a sport 🌐 Tell children about yourself and what you did at their age 🌐 Treat the kids equally 🌐 Attend recitals, sports events, performances, etc. 🌐 Attend school events for kids 🌐 Attend parent–teacher conferences 🌐 Review daily homework 🌐 Monitor and support homework plan 🌐 Fill out school paperwork	N	S

CATEGORY	NEEDS AND WANTS	I/N	S/D
	🌐 Review report cards 🌐 Make school lunches 🌐 Share school drop-off and pickup 🌐 Schedule children's playdates 🌐 Schedule doctor appointments 🌐 Schedule dentist appointments 🌐 Take kids to appointments 🌐 Share appointment follow-up (pick up prescriptions, schedule next visit, etc.) 🌐 Shop for kids' clothes 🌐 Shop for kids' shoes 🌐 Schedule kids' haircuts 🌐 Monitor kids' chores 🌐 Pay allowance 🌐 Help arrange child care		
CELEBRATE: Become a Believer in Ritual	🌐 Help plan birthday parties 🌐 Help pick out and wrap birthday gifts 🌐 Attend children's birthday parties and participate in games 🌐 Help pick out Halloween costumes 🌐 Participate in pumpkin carving 🌐 Help pick out and address holiday cards 🌐 Sign cards with your own name 🌐 Help shop for gifts 🌐 Help wrap, pack, and mail presents as necessary	I	S

CATEGORY	NEEDS AND WANTS	I/N	S/D
	⊕ Help build family gingerbread house ⊕ Attend holiday events with family ⊕ Help be Santa Claus ⊕ Help decorate Christmas tree (or hide the afikomen) ⊕ Help make valentines with kids ⊕ Help decorate Easter eggs with kids ⊕ Help make Easter baskets ⊕ Help be the Easter bunny ⊕ Help ensure the family eats together		
PLAY: **Become** **My Lover**	⊕ Get marriage counseling ⊕ Take me on dates once in a while ⊕ Occasionally dress like you're going to a job interview (and I'm the one in charge of hiring) ⊕ Don't turn every back rub into sex ⊕ Remember that I have feelings, too ⊕ Don't criticize me all the time ⊕ Pay attention to what I like ⊕ Pay attention to what I say ⊕ Pay attention to what I do ⊕ Pay attention to what I need ⊕ Respect what I don't like and don't want ⊕ Don't make unilateral decisions. Remember that we have a partnership.	N	S

CATEGORY	NEEDS AND WANTS	I/N	S/D
	⚫ Show interest in my work and my life as an individual ⚫ Don't take out your anger about other problems on me		
SHARE: **Become a** **Domestic God**	⚫ Help with grocery shopping ⚫ Help shop for household supplies ⚫ Help with meal planning ⚫ Share the cooking ⚫ Share the dish washing ⚫ Help do the laundry ⚫ Pick up and drop off dry cleaning ⚫ Help maintain family car (fill with gas, get oil changed, get car cleaned) ⚫ Share the housecleaning chores ⚫ Share the yard work ⚫ Participate in house decorating decisions ⚫ Help to buy furniture ⚫ Take pets for vet visits	N	D
PLAN: **Become** **Fiscally** **Responsible**	⚫ Share responsibility for paying bills ⚫ Help with tax filings and payments ⚫ Stop paying ATM fees ⚫ Set priorities and take care of financial obligations before buying luxuries	N	D

CATEGORY	NEEDS AND WANTS	I/N	S/D
	⊕ Discuss and agree on discretionary spending with your partner		
	⊕ Create a joint savings plan		
	⊕ Establish financial goals together		
	⊕ Pay-off-debt plan		
	⊕ Create college savings plan		
	⊕ Create retirement plan		
	⊕ Organized approach for record keeping		
	⊕ Help plan family vacations		
	⊕ Help plan holiday travel		
	⊕ Help determine and work toward long-term family goals		
	⊕ Participate in insurance decisions		
	⊕ Help decide investment planning and strategy		
	⊕ Participate in drafting a will		
EVOLVE: Become the Man You Want to Be	⊕ Find a therapist	I	S
	⊕ Get into therapy and stay with it		
	⊕ Confront difficult issues		
	⊕ Manage mental health benefits and filings under your benefits plan		
	⊕ Get appropriate medication for depression or anxiety		
	⊕ Be honest with yourself		

CATEGORY	NEEDS AND WANTS	I/N	S/D
	⚙ Stop blaming others for your unhappiness ⚙ Reevaluate your spiritual or religious life ⚙ Don't self-medicate with drugs or alcohol ⚙ Stop smoking ⚙ Exercise ⚙ Take responsibility for your own happiness		

STEP FIVE: Chart your categories in the following four-block chart and find your focus.

For each of the nine areas, you should now "chart" each category. The vertical axis corresponds with the importance level of each area and the horizontal axis corresponds with how well you're doing in each area.

This is called a *four-block*—but we also call it the Relationship Map, because that's exactly what it is: a tool for navigating your relationship, knowing where you are and where you want to be. This is a quick and easy way to see what you should focus on. As we mentioned before, we know that when you deal with everything at once, it can be a bit overwhelming. When all is said and done, every area in the relationship will be charted and will fall into one of four categories.

	★ MY RELATIONSHIP MAP ★	

LEVEL OF DISSATISFACTION

High

ND

Not so important
I am dissatisfied.

Example:
—Share
—Plan

ID

Important
I am dissatisfied.
(This is the stuff that
makes you the craziest.)

Example:
—Communicate
—Deal

NS

Not so important
I am satisfied.

Example:
—Love (if you don't have children
    this wouldn't be an issue)
—Play

IS

Important
I am satisfied.
(Count your blessings.
Think about the things
in this box when you need
to feel good!)

Example:
—Work
—Celebrate
—Evolve

Low

Low   **IMPORTANCE**   **High**

Now you can see, graphically, which issues to focus on. Concentrate on those issues, and those chapters, which end up in the top right-hand quadrant of our chart. These are the issues that you rate high in importance, and high in dissatisfaction, and these are the problems that are causing you the most anxiety. We are going to use the four-block in various guises throughout this book. At the end of each charting process, you'll know EXACTLY how important certain issues are to you.

✳ In Each Chapter ✳

Dying to make lots of changes in your husband and your marriage? Do not become overwhelmed. If you become overwhelmed, you'll become paralyzed—and end up changing nothing.

At the beginning of each chapter we've created a series of exercises you can do to prioritize. First, we give you our Scorecard—but many of you will make your own. The idea is to winnow down the areas of your life that you're working on so that you can concentrate on the items that are most important.

For example: Let's say you are reading our chapter on fatherhood. You have identified for yourself thirty aspects of being a good dad.

Step One—Prioritize: You fill in your four-block chart with the needs/wants that correspond with the category, to identify which of those thirty items are of highest priority for you—the items in the upper right-hand quadrant of highest importance and greatest dissatisfaction:

LEVEL OF DISSATISFACTION

	ND		**ID**
	• Make school lunches • Volunteer at school when required • Schedule doctor appointments • Schedule dentist appointments • Take kids to appointments • Fill out school paperwork • Play with kids every day • Tell children about yourself and what you did at their age		• Treat the kids equally • Talk to your children individually at least once a day • Keep track of what they're doing, thinking, and feeling • Go to movies and on other family outings • Read to kids every night • Monitor and support homework plan • Review daily homework • Monitor kids' chores • Teach each kid a sport • Help arrange childcare
	NS		**IS**
	• Shop for kids' clothes • Shop for kids' shoes • Schedule kids' haircuts • Share school drop-off and pickup • Schedule children's playdates • Take kids to the park • Go on bike rides with kids • Share appointment follow-up (pick up prescriptions, schedule next visit, etc.) • Pay allowance • Take kids to parties and other engagements		• Attend recitals, sports events, performances, etc. • Attend school events for kids • Attend parent–teacher conferences • Review report cards • Help to arrange after-school schedule • Help to schedule kids' sports and lessons

IMPORTANCE

Now let's say you rank ten of those items as being of highest importance and greatest dissatisfaction. Ten items are A LOT to work on. So let's continue prioritizing. Essentially, you need to ask yourself: What can I change—and what do I need my mate to help us change?

STEP TWO—Filter: Take the items in the upper right quadrant of the four-block. For each item, ask:

Can I fix this myself? (And if the answer is yes):

- Is there a one-time fix to this issue?
- Can I fix this with technology or a new product that is on the market?

Set aside those items you can handle. All others—continue to step three.

STEP THREE—Analyze: For items that remain, you'll need to develop an approach to fixing them. Determine whether an item is going to be easy or hard to fix by asking yourself the following questions:

- Is my husband going to be cooperative on this issue?
- Do we (my husband or I) have the skills necessary to properly address this issue?
- Has this been an issue for less than one year?
- Can the task be done by only one person?

If you answered "yes" to all of these—we would call your problem easy, if you answered "no" to any of the questions—your problem would be considered hard.

For Easy Problems: We recommend approaching your husband with a recommendation and a quick conversation.

For Hard Problems: We recommend that if your husband isn't cooperative, prep work may be needed in order to gain buy-in, that is, agreement or compliance. (Each chapter will help you with gaining your mate's cooperation on a myriad of topics.) If neither of you has the skill set, you may need to seek outside help, go to training, or pay someone else to do it. If it's a problem that's been on the list for a long time and it's going to take both of you to do it—we may recommend Project Planning (see chapter 2, for instance).

(Note: We recommend you handle the easy things first— you'll be more motivated to progress to the harder issues if you see the rewards of fixing the easier ones first.)

STEP FOUR—Plan Your Approach: These fundamental rules will help you no matter which chapter of the book/area of your life you focus on first. We will be exploring them time and again throughout the book.

Communicate: There are four key components to excellent communication: *honesty, clarity, good timing,* and *staying on message* (that is, pitching the appropriate message to the right audience). Nowhere is this more true than when you're talking to the person you need to communicate with most: your husband. We have devoted all of chapter 1 to the importance of communication.

Be Creative: As soon as you think there's only one solution to a problem and you have it—that is usually the sign that there are many solutions. Being open to novel ideas—even when they are not yours—is one of the hallmarks of being a successful executive . . . and, we realize now, is equally important in the home. It's pleasant to think that there is one person (you) who has the vision to come up with the perfect solution to lead the troops (the family). But the reality is, very often at work, solutions come out of brainstorming sessions where team members (the family) all contribute. Believe us: There is never one person at work—*or at home*—who always has the best idea.

Assign Roles and Responsibilities: Yeah, we know, you thought this was going to be all about HIM changing. In fact, this is as much about your change as his. For a team to be successful— everyone has to be committed to the goals. This means that you can't just "manage" him from the sidelines—you have to be a player, not just a coach. It could be that you've been doing the chores you preferred because you were assigning the roles and responsibilities. Participation in the decision-making process is the most effective way to gain cooperation and buy-in. Just as you have preferences, so does your partner, so part of assigning roles and responsibilities is about understanding where preferences can be leveraged. If you are responsible for things you like to do, you are also much more open to negotiation around the things you don't like to do.

Measure the Results/Progress: We encourage you to measure and track your progress. The idea is to measure your progress as objectively as possible—and be able to show the progress, if you like, to your mate. Why? Well, if you've ever seen the movie *Rashômon*—where a heinous crime is witnessed by four different people, each of whom has an entirely different story about what happened—you know how easy it is to view an event in many different ways. It's not foolproof, of course, but our standard of measurement will help you stop second-guessing yourself.

Once you've completed each chapter, it's time to be honest.

We assume you'll take some time to digest and implement some of our suggestions. Then, after some period of time has gone by, we hope you'll revisit the relevant chapter and ask yourself:

- What worked?
- What didn't?
- Would you change anything?
- Do you hold up your end of the bargain?
- Does he?

And remember: Constant refinements are necessary to keep a marriage happy. We will discuss these refinements in our final chapter.

CHAPTER 1

Communicate

Become My Friend

• • • • •

Don't have sex, man. It leads to kissing
and pretty soon you have to start talking to them.

—STEVE MARTIN

You know what's usually the first thing to die when a marriage goes south? Friendship. Not love, not sex; *liking*. You find you don't like each other much anymore. And for the most part, you don't like each other because you've forgotten how to speak to each other.

OUR SCORECARD FOR COMMUNICATING

···

- Talk about what you're thinking and feeling; share your opinions and preferences
- Speak your mind in an honest and constructive way
- Open up about what's bothering you
- DON'T YELL!!!!
- Keep me apprised of what's going on in your life

- **Don't make unilateral decisions. Remember that we have a partnership.**
- **Show interest in my work and my life as an individual**
- **Don't take out your anger about other problems on me**

....

* Yakety-Yak, Please Talk Back: *
Your Scorecard

STEP ONE—Prioritize: List all the essentials of communication you'd like in your marriage. Fill them in on their proper places on your four-block chart, identifying which items are high and low priority for you, and which items you're satisfied with and not satisfied with. Here's what our Relationship Map for communication looked like:

* OUR RELATIONSHIP MAP: COMMUNICATION *	
ND	**ID**
• Share your opinions and preferences • Speak your mind in an honest and constructive way • Remember that we have a partnership.	• DON'T YELL!!!! • Don't take out your anger about other problems on me. • Don't make unilateral decisions. • Keep me apprised of what's going on in your life
NS	**IS**
• Open up about what's bothering you • Talk about what you're thinking and feeling	• Show interest in my work and my life as an individual

LEVEL OF DISSATISFACTION

IMPORTANCE

STEP TWO—Filter: Take the items in the upper right quadrant of your four-block—the items of highest importance and greatest dissatisfaction.

For each item, ask:

- Is there a one-time fix to this issue? For example, a communication board or location for everyone to post notes or place reminders for others to see?
- Can I fix this with technology or a new product that is on the market? (For example: Husband forgets to tell you things? How about a portable pocket recorder for his commute?)

These are the items you can handle. Set them aside. For all others in the upper right-hand quadrant, continue to step three.

STEP THREE—Analyze: For items that remain, you'll need to develop an approach to fixing them. Determine whether an item is going to be easy or hard to fix by asking yourself the following questions:

- Is my husband going to be cooperative on this issue? (There are some issues that might be solved by a well-planned conversation, but others where you know that your partner will be entrenched in his point of view, custom, or cultural perspective.)
- Do we (my husband or I) have the skills necessary to properly address this issue?
- Has this been an issue for less than one year?
- Can the task be done by only one person?

If you answered "yes" to all of these—we would call your problem easy. If you answered "no" to any of the questions—your problem would be considered hard.

For Easy Problems: We recommend approaching your husband with a recommendation and a quick conversation. He may have no clue that you feel you're not getting through to him.

For Hard Problems: If your husband isn't cooperative, prep work may be needed in order to gain agreement or compliance. If neither of you has the skill set, you may need to go to training or pay someone else to do it (perhaps communication classes, or therapy/counseling for both parties).

STEP FOUR—Plan Your Approach: Julie and Phillip, for example, had an exceedingly noisy household. And the noisier it got, the more people tuned one another out. They realized that the shouting that took place during actual fights was in fact a symptom of a larger familial problem: Everyone, both kids and adults, got louder in response to the sense that they were not being heard. (And they weren't.) It was a tough problem for them, and one that still plagues them, but essentially what they did was this: ban shouting *entirely*, even when it was just a question of someone shouting a question from upstairs to someone downstairs. They also banned all talking over the TV—and banned the TV being on any time *except* when people were actively watching. (They realized that the TV had just become this wall of sound that was an annoying background accompaniment to everything.)

So after much discussion—some of it heated—they instituted this rule: No one has to answer a question when a voice is raised. But a question *has* to be answered when it's said in a normal tone of voice. This took some practice—and it's definitely still a work in progress. But it's made the decibel level of the house quieter, and the discourse infinitely more civil.

(Note: We recommend tackling the easy issues first—you'll be more motivated to progress to the harder issues if you see the rewards of fixing the easier ones first.)

CORE STRATEGIES FOR SUCCESS:
Honesty
Clarity
The Right Message
The Right Timing

Let's face it: To say you want your husband to communicate doesn't mean that if you married Stanley Kowalski you expect him to become Oscar Wilde. In fact, many of us married men we thought of as "the strong, silent type." We associate those qualities with depth, with seriousness. Unfortunately, just as a cigar is sometimes just a cigar, sometimes an uncommunicative guy is not so much deep as someone who just doesn't want to put out the effort to explain himself—or understand you.

This is very difficult for the average woman to wrap her mind around. What's so tough about discussing your feelings? But in this culture, from the earliest age, when it comes to self-expression we have very different expectations of boys and girls. A recent study at the University of Missouri wanted to see whether men appear less sensitive than girls because they want to project strength, or can't handle embarrassment. Turns out that's not quite the case—in fact, that explanation is too emotion-laden. Young boys do not open up NOT because they want to be perceived as "strong," but simply because they thought emotional discussions were a waste of time. They just don't think discussing problems leads to a *solution* to those problems.

On the other hand, not only are women expected to discuss their feelings and provide comfort to others, we tend to think something's wrong with them if they don't. In 2005, research teams at Purdue University and the University of Minnesota conducted two experiments. In the first, 137 participants answered questions about stories they read that described men and women giving ineffective comforting messages to people in need—that is, instead of just listening and offering sympathy, they gave advice. (Advice, unless explicitly requested, is rarely comforting. Most women instinctively understand this. Most men don't.) In the second study, forty-four men and forty-three women discussed an upsetting event with either a female or male comforter who also used ineffective comforting messages. Both experiments found that women did not like female comforters who used ineffective messages as much as they liked male comforters who used the same messages. In contrast, men equally liked the female and male helpers. Basically, these studies show that we hold women to a higher standard than men when it comes to a prime form of communication: providing solace in hard times.

Not to say that women's endless dissection of feelings is always such a great thing. But if many of us waste time by talking, many men waste *lives* by not talking. The end of a marriage, we discovered, is often preceded by a long silence. Before anything concrete happened to devastate our marriages, we both watched as our ability talk to our husbands slowly deteriorated. We ended up talking AT them and not TO them. Dave and Donna, in particular, never communicated well—not because Dave didn't want to, but because he had trouble identifying for himself what troubled him. He was not a big talker to begin with. So verbalizing what bothered him was completely out of the question.

This lack of communication was really the root of their problems. Donna would have preferred if she and Dave were like James Carville and Mary Matalin: two people constantly arguing over diametrically opposed viewpoints they could not reconcile, rather than the situation they had—which was Donna shouting into the wind. She was constantly talking, seeking feedback, and trying to fix things, while Dave sat mute. He could go for several days in almost-complete silence. Their children would walk on eggshells, terrified of setting him off. Actually, at times in the past Donna actually *tried* to set him off, just to ease the tension. But eventually she got tired of begging for a response. At that point, everything that happened between them dwelt in the Land of Not My Problem: If he wouldn't talk, she would shut down.

This was the beginning of the end for them. Donna was not going to be responsible for Dave's lack of participation; she was not going to be responsible for trying to fix something that he had no interest in fixing, and she was not going to let it ruin her life. They began to go days without uttering a word to each other. They became strangers.

In our jobs Donna and I spend a lot of time thinking about effective communication: how we can get what we want and need, while still making the people around us feel engaged and motivated and not merely bossed around. If we had any hopes of saving our marriages (and remember, for the longest time we didn't) we knew we'd have to apply similarly canny strategies. And we'd have to improve the level of discourse beyond what it was when we were at our worst, which was something like this:

"Screw you."
"Yeah? Well, screw YOU."

It sounds so easy, yet it can be even more difficult to learn how to talk again than to learn how to make love. But we found some techniques that worked. When someone asks us what's the biggest change in our marriages since our husbands left the house, we answer: They talk!

Here are our Golden Rules of Gab:

No Pussyfooting Around: A study published in a 2005 *Journal of Personality and Social Psychology* by University of Toledo psychologist Lisa Neff showed that women say they are more responsive to their husbands' stress than vice versa. Are they?

It turns out that under lab conditions, the husbands were as comforting and supportive as their wives. At home, though, the story was different. The problem, Neff suggests, may lie not with the "clueless" husband but with the wife. Much research suggests that women have roundabout ways of telling their partners what they need. Since women are generally better at reading nonverbal cues, they are dumbfounded—and disappointed—when their husbands don't pick up on theirs.

Many of us foolishly equate love with the ability to read our minds. But we've learned from years of experience: You can love someone and not have a clue what they want. If we don't say exactly what we want and how we want it, we won't get it.

Donna used to make generalized requests of Dave like

"Please take out the trash," and he would say, "Sure." What she meant was, "Please take out the trash in the next fifteen minutes because I'm cleaning and I'd like to be done so I can go do something fun." What he heard was, "Please take out the trash sometime this weekend." So she would become frustrated if the trash was not gone in her time frame—a time frame that, of course, she never bothered to mention.

This type of unstated expectation was a regular occurrence with Donna and Dave that often lead to a climate of bickering and general annoyance. As Donna learned to frame her requests specifically, clearly communicating her expectations, the bickering died down. Additionally, there were times when Dave could not or would not meet her expectation—but because the communication was clear, Donna could then make another plan. Take the trash-removal scenario: If Donna asked Dave to take out the trash in the next fifteen minutes, but Dave was otherwise occupied and said no, then rather than being upset Donna could either take out the trash herself, or she could modify her expectation. Perhaps Dave could take it out when he was done with whatever was occupying his attention and it would be satisfactory.

On the "Focus on Families" Web site, a recent article entitled "Husbands Are Hunters, Wives Are Hinters" got our attention. The gist of the article was that when it comes to gifts (and just about everything else), wives hint about what they want and hope husbands will get it. Husbands, the hunters, want to be told simply and directly, with no guessing, so they can shoot it down and drag it home.

Timing Is Everything: Want to make sure your employee hates you? Hand him a huge complicated project on Friday evening, around 4:55 PM—then tell him you want him to think about it over the weekend, and you'll talk on Monday. If you wanted results, you wouldn't do that, would you? (The same person, given the project on Monday or Tuesday, might very well attack it with vigor.) Nor would you wait till the eve of a large bonus decision to tell your boss that you want to take two weeks of vacation.

We all have times when we're more amenable to doing something unpleasant than at other times. The chances of your getting your husband to fix the sink in the middle of his Sunday games is pretty much negligible. And, as one of our girlfriends tells us, "If my husband wants something from me—anything—first thing in the morning, he'd better be holding a Starbucks latte in his hands."

So ask yourself: When is he going to be at his best to hear what I'm saying? If he's most relaxed after dinner, maybe that's the best time to bring up the fact that there's a play on Tuesday afternoon and he needs to leave work early, instead of lunging at him with your requests the moment he gets through the door.

Speak His Language: Make sure that when you communicate you are using appropriate terminology and techniques, because sometimes our language confuses more than it clarifies.

Julie and Phillip often seemed to be talking to each other in different languages. When he said to her, for example, "It's taken care of," she assumed that meant, "I took care of it," because that's what it would mean if she said it. But she began to realize that that phrase had a host of meanings. It was Phillip's job, for example, to get their daughter Madelyn to school, and she'd always been assured that it had been taken care of. One day, she was off work and decided to take their daughter herself.

"You'd better tell Barb," Phil said. Barb? Barb was the next-door neighbor. Why did Julie need to tell Barb?

Well, apparently, Barb had been taking Madelyn to school for the past month. (She had offered shortly after Phillip and Julie's son was born because their children went to the same school and she didn't want Phillip to have to bundle the baby in the winter for such a short trip.) Julie was aghast. Why did her neighbor know more about her child's itinerary than she did? And did Barb think Julie was an ingrate, never calling to say thanks?

Today, Julie is VERY clear about the question she's asking, and she makes sure Phillip is very clear about the answer he's giving (and vice versa). They work hard to keep each other in the loop. As much as she loves and trusts her husband, Julie frets that one day she's going to ask him, "Did you call the babysitter?" and he'll reply, "It's taken care of," and she'll come back home to find her children minded by that rottweiler that's in the *Good Dog, Carl* series.

Choosing the wrong language can also land us in needless power struggles, both at work and home. Most of us who work in corporate settings have had the experience of giving a boss a brilliant idea . . . and having that idea ignored. Then, a colleague will pass along that same idea but subtly convey that she was inspired by something the boss had said in the first place . . . suddenly, your old stinky idea becomes someone else's stroke of genius. Annoying, but also very human: We are most attached to the ideas we think we came up with ourselves or at least contributed to in some way. Therein lies the "upsell": Your husband will not only buy what you're selling, but he will buy *more* of it, if he sees its advantages not just to the family but to himself personally.

So if, say, you need a new car, and there's any way to convince him that the car you want is one that *he* noticed first, or has a DVD player/navigation system/dopey pointless gadget that *he* thought was essential . . . the chances of winning him over to your make and model are excellent.

Know What's Important to Him: Have you been making incorrect assumptions about what matters to him that make you misinterpret each other? There are times in business when a very minor, inexpensive concession that was not in the budget—an ergonomic chair, let's say, or a particular kind of computer mouse—can make the difference between happiness and secret resentment for an employee. And the same holds true for our spouses, as Julie's story illustrates.

Phillip has large feet—size 14. For years, I've been obsessed with the fact that I don't think the size 11–13 socks that are widely available fit him properly. So for years, every time I went into a shoe store or department store of ANY kind, I checked for size 14 socks. I never found them, but still I lived in hope.

Fast forward to 2005. I went to Wisconsin to go outlet shopping with one of my daughters. I stumbled upon a Big and Tall men's store and wandered in. They have the socks— size 14. I feel like I've won the lottery and buy some twenty pairs—a few of each type, so he can luxuriate in the feeling of well-being that comes from socks that fit properly. Plus: Now he will know how much I love him!

On the way home I get lost and become Road Rage Girl: Outta my way, woman with perfect socks coming through! I'm now somewhere lost in downtown Chicago and have to make it home by 3:30 to pick up my other daughter from an event. I finally get home, breathless and seething with fury, and practically throw the socks at him and ask him to put them on. He says he doesn't have time. He barely looks at the socks.

WHAT?

But . . . but . . . but . . . I want him to try the socks on NOW. I launch into a harangue that begins with the past few hours and escalates until I am reiterating his innumerable transgressions over the past few years. Teeth gritted, I describe how much of my life I've now invested in making sure his big stinky canoe feet are comfortable, and today is the culmination of years of sacrifice. He refuses to put on the socks and leaves the house without them. I am beside myself. I pray none of the neighbors sees me following him out the door, screaming about socks.

Now, Phillip had been planning forever to do some landscaping in the front of the house. Finally—the first week of June—I told him we had enough cash for him to get the supplies he needed to get started. He got the supplies and started working furiously on laying bricks. When he finished, the bricks on either side of the pathway were not symmetrical. He undid one side and started over—a huge undertaking. When he finished again, he asked how they looked. "Fine," I said, absentmindedly. He asked again. "Great, fine, whatever— they're bricks." The third time he asked I shot back, "How are the socks?" To which he replied, "The socks are good, but how do you like the bricks?" and I said, "The bricks look good, but how do you like the socks?" This went on for a while, till we were both giggling.

The point was: We were both trying SO HARD to impress

each other that we didn't realize what the other one was try-ing to do for their beloved. It all comes back to feedback and recognition. I didn't realize until that moment that it was AS IMPORTANT for Phillip to hear about the bricks as it was for me to hear about the socks.

If You Ask for Your Man's Opinion, You Have to Actually Pay Attention to It: Phillip is a man of many opinions. Yet when Julie asked him what he thought, the answer was generally "I don't care" or "You decide." This drove her berserk—and never stopped him, of course, from making comments later like "I knew that color wouldn't work" or "It was up to you—if it doesn't work, it's your fault."

It took a long time for Julie to admit to herself that part of the reason Phillip fobbed off the decision on her was that, when he did give an opinion, if she disagreed she would blithely ig-nore him. And the less input he gave . . . well, the easier her decision-making process was.

Julie also had to learn that if she wanted to get more than a curt answer, she had to listen to Phillip carefully—had to pay at-tention to the details and stop asking him questions in multiple-choice format. (Go ahead, try it some time: You get monosyllabic answers. A friend of ours had to interview the famously terse Brad Pitt for a magazine, and just to get any response from him, she began to give him choices in this format: A, B, C, D. By the end of the interview, Pitt was practically grunting. This was not her finest hour as a journalist.)

These days, we both make sure that when we ask our hus-bands' opinions, it's because we actually want to know. If we don't want to know, we don't ask. This was a hard message to get across, but now they know we're serious. And if either says, "I don't care," we know it's not a phrase that means "I'm not telling you, because you'll go and do what you want anyway." It means, simply, "I don't care." There's no hidden agenda.

Turn Nagging Into Bragging: It works if you're four or forty: Assume the best instead of the worst about a person's intentions, and that person's behavior will often meet your expectations.

This is hard to admit, but . . . over time, we had become nags. "Why didn't you do X?" "Why didn't you do Y?" True, our nagging was sometimes warranted. But our well-honed technique of being gnats in our husbands' ears wasn't working. We had to unlearn that behavior. Instead of catching him screwing up, we had to learn to catch him doing something right . . . then praise him to the skies for it.

Reinforcement and recognition of good behavior instead of constant criticism of bad behavior leads to the desire to repeat the good behavior, however minor the improved behavior is. This is why so many organizations have Employee-of-the-Week programs, where the reward consists of nothing more than the employee's picture hung up prominently someplace (and, in certain businesses, like telemarketing, a small cash or prize bonus). Sure, in some high-stakes businesses huge bonuses come but once a year. But the employee's attitude can't be, "Oh, I can slack off eleven months of the year, then work hard for one month." (The spousal equivalent statement: "I can be a jerk most of the time, then buy her a big birthday present.")

We actually think through what we say now. This means one of two things: 1) We don't comment on the negative at all because the positive far outweighs it; or 2) we acknowledge the good even before we discuss the bad. There is no value in pointing out small imperfections in the work Phillip and Dave do for the family. It doesn't make anyone feel better and, in fact, doesn't address any real issues.

Ban Both Pouting AND Shouting: During the worst days of our marriages, we often thought of that well-known saying by the author Ambrose Bierce: "Speak when you are angry and you will make the best speech you will ever regret." Our communication generally alternated between silence and screaming. Maybe guys don't think of it as silence. Maybe they think of it as "reconnaissance ignoring" or something. Whatever it is, most women hate it; they want issues hashed out, and silence seems deeply hostile. Screaming is actually better, except for the fact that it terrifies the children and pets. What's particularly awful about this pout/shout cycle is that the most minute problems can become earth-shattering, a new chapter in the book you're writing called *How Did I Ever End Up Married to This Putz?* Making scratches in the new wood floors or not taking out the trash suddenly becomes a bigger deal than it should be. You think, "I married someone who is unthinking and careless of my feelings"—not "What can I put on the wood to avoid the scratches?" or "How can I help him remember to take out the trash?" The normal ebbs and flows of a relationship suddenly become needlessly dramatic.

It's not as if we've given up yelling entirely. But every time we find ourselves sulking or shouting, we make an appointment—an actual calendar date—to try to find a long-term fix to the short-term problem. There isn't a fix to everything. But we've found we have cut down on the pout/shout cycle by about 75 percent. Knowing that we will at least try to find a solution, even if that's a few days in the future, allows us to calm down and act like reasonable humans again.

Stay on Message, and Speak to Him as Politely as You Speak to Your Friends: We can't emphasize this enough. While the message itself is the most important part of any discussion, we often get lazy in our home conversations. We find ourselves being more polite and considerate to complete strangers that we are to our families. The next time you want to say something—think about what message it is that you'd like to deliver, then focus on the fact that you want it to be accepted positively.

If there is one area of our lives that will always be a work in progress, it is here, in our ability to talk to each other without hostility and false assumptions, with kindness and caring and trust. Sometimes it is hard. Always it is foundational—a "must have" in our four-block.

It's not only that our husbands are better talkers now—though they are. It's that we are both better and more eager listeners.

CHAPTER 2

Deal

Become Self-sufficient

• • • • •

Man must cease attributing his problems
to his environment, and learn again
to exercise his will—his personal responsibility.

—ALBERT SCHWEITZER

"Mommy."
"Mommy."
"Mom-EEEEE."

We laugh and put up with the constant demands of our kids. But
you know when it's not so funny? When that "kid" is the man on
the other side of the bed. When that hunka-hunka burning love
is sulking on the couch without a job (or with one he hates) . . .
without domestic skills . . . without pretty much anything except
an appetite for beer, sex, and pizza.

It's shockingly easy to become a mommy to your man. At the
beginning of many marriages, it seems the right thing to do,
too. After all, he's just a big baby who can't help himself, right?

And as we became more and more the classic "enablers," picking up the crumbs after our husbands stepped on the cookie, we found ourselves living with men who could no more fend for themselves than our elementary-school-age children. (No, we take that back; even our tots knew how to empty the dishwasher.)

OUR SCORECARD FOR SELF-SUFFICIENCY

- Rent an apartment, schedule move, pack belongings, and haul away your stuff
- Arrange for gas and electricity
- Get telephone and cable
- Help prepare children for your move
- Transfer accounts and make change-of-address notifications
- Set up your own bank accounts
- Balance your own checkbook
- Get your own credit cards
- Get your own home insurance
- Get your own car insurance
- Maintain your own car
- Furnish your own home
- Make your home appropriate and comfortable for children (toys, etc.)
- Select your own doctors and dentist
- Make your own appointments
- Follow through with doctors' recommendations
- Read and understand your own benefit plans
- File your own insurance paperwork
- Pay your own bills

- **Buy your own groceries**
- **Make your own meals**
- **Clean up after yourself**
- **Do your own laundry**

⁎ "Be a Grown-up": ⁎
Your Scorecard

STEP ONE—Prioritize: List all the essentials of being an adult that you'd like to see in your marriage. (You'll note our list included many that, we hope, won't pertain to you—because they involved getting our men to leave the house.) Fill them in on their proper place on your four-block chart, identifying which items are of highest priority for you.

⁎ OUR RELATIONSHIP MAP: SELF SUFFICIENCY ⁎

LEVEL OF DISSATISFACTION

ND
- Select your own doctors and dentist
- Make your own appointments
- Follow through with doctors' recommendations
- Read and understand your own benefit plans
- File your own insurance paperwork
- Maximize your benefits and observe compliance requirements

ID
- Set up your own bank accounts
- Balance your own checkbook
- Get your own credit cards
- Get your own home insurance
- Get your own car insurance
- Maintain your own car
- Furnish your own home
- Make your home appropriate and comfortable for children (toys, etc.)
- Pay your own bills

IMPORTANCE

	NS		**IS**

LEVEL OF DISSATISFACTION

NS	IS
• Rent an apartment	• Buy your own groceries
• Haul away your stuff	• Make your own meals
• Arrange for gas and electricity	• Clean up after yourself
• Get telephone and cable	• Do your own laundry
• Help prepare children for your	• Rent an apartment
move	• Arrange for gas and electricity
• Pack your belongings	• Get telephone and cable
• Schedule move	
• Transfer accounts and make	
change-of-address notifications	

IMPORTANCE

STEP TWO—Filter: Take the items in the upper right quadrant of your four-block—the items of highest importance and greatest dissatisfaction.

For each item, ask:

- Is there a one-time fix to this issue? (That is, he's not self-sufficient here, but I can solve the problem and it's really no biggie.)
- Can I fix this with technology or a new product that is on the market? (For example: You and your husband both hate grocery shopping, particularly the lugging of heavy items. But as averse as he is to brick-and-mortar shopping, he'll cooperate with anything that involves a computer and a mouse. Solution: You sign up for an online grocer in your area such as www.yourgrocer.com or www.freshdirect.com, one of you buys, and the other puts away. Both of you can

shop—and moreover, you can shop from work. Problem solved.)

These are the items you can handle. Set them aside. For all others in the upper right-hand quadrant, continue to step three.

STEP THREE—Analyze: For items that remain, you'll need to develop an approach to fixing them. Determine whether an item is going to be easy or hard to fix by asking yourself the following questions:

- Is my husband going to be cooperative on this issue? (There are some issues that might be solved by a well-planned conversation, but others where you know that your partner will be entrenched in his point of view, custom, or cultural perspective.)
- Do we (my husband or I) have the skills necessary to properly address this issue?
- Has this been an issue for less than one year?
- Can the task be done by only one person?

If you answered "yes" to all of these—we would call your problem easy. If you answered "no" to any of the questions—your problem would be considered hard.

For Easy Problems: We recommend approaching your husband with a recommendation and a quick conversation. It's possible, for example, that he's not averse to balancing a checkbook—but no one's ever shown him how.

For Hard Problems: We recommend that if your husband

isn't cooperative, prep work may be needed in order to gain agreement or compliance. If neither of you has the skill set, you may need to go to training or pay someone else to do it (counseling, financial planning, a course at a community college).

STEP FOUR—**Plan Your Approach:** For us, many of the difficult problems could only be solved one way: Bite the bullet and stop enabling. When Julie wanted Phillip to get his own bank account, the only way she could make that happen was to remove his name from her bank account (which she could do, since she was the person who had opened it), and face his anger when he suddenly found himself with a paycheck in his hands that he couldn't convert into dollars. The trick here is: Be prepared for the aftermath—and for repercussions. Because once you've made a decision to cut him off at the knees, you can't wimp out. He'll never take you seriously again.

> **CORE STRATEGIES FOR SUCCESS:**
> **No Enabling**
> **Project Planning**

How did we find ourselves with husbands who were infantilized? Well, their incessant plaint used to be "I've never done it before," "You're better at it than I am," or "I don't know how to do it." Which is hooey. Did we take a class in how to be a grown-up? No, because that class doesn't exist. All of us have to learn things through trial and error.

At the same time, most women, when they get into a situation like ours, have to struggle with a problem men don't need to battle quite as strenuously: empathy. Many of us also have an inborn desire to support our husbands in a separation, stemming from our sister-feelings toward women who've been homemakers and then have been left without money or position after divorce. Both Julie and Donna had a lot of sympathy for their husbands' financial plight; after all, Donna's husband, Dave, had volunteered to stay home with the kids instead of working, so how could he just be shoved out the door without any financial help?

On the other hand, in our desire to be equitable and "nice," many of us lose sight of what "niceness" actually means. Is it nice to be a martyr and make someone we love both helpless and resentful? Because that's what a martyr does—and that's what we were doing.

Let us reiterate: The problems in our marriages were extreme. But we're not going to gloss over our problems because we think they're unique, that no one can relate to them, that the big problem in most marriages is nothing more than the man forgetting to put batteries in the remote. When a marriage dissolves into the forced departure of a spouse from the house, the root cause is always something serious—such as drinking, or depression, or infidelity. Or physical abuse, financial irresponsibility, gambling, total incommunicativeness, emotional abandonment, drug addiction, or mental instability. These are the types of problems that often lead a man into becoming a less-than-full citizen in FamilyLand USA.

The larger problems can devastate our lives; the smaller ones just put us on the slow train to Crazy Town. How many times have you vented to a girlfriend about his inability to balance a checkbook or flush the toilet?

That said, we understand that many readers will not find themselves with husbands so infantilized that they have no clue how to open their own bank accounts or understand their own health insurance policies. Their husbands may not have problems that so thoroughly cloud their ability to think and act for themselves. However, we hope our own examples can be applied to your (hopefully) less extreme circumstances. We're 99 percent sure that every wife wants her husband to improve his self-sufficiency just a bit, whether that means cooking dinner for the family or managing the shopping.

For those readers who *do* find themselves in similarly dire straits, we're here to serve. So this chapter, which may cause a few eyes to roll (Who doesn't know how to do *that*?) is nevertheless essential to many of us.

As a human resources leader, Donna has the unpleasant task of firing wayward employees. There is a wide range of reactions to getting the ax. Shouting is commonplace; hitting not unknown. One person went on a campaign with senior executives (phone calls, e-mails, letters, etc.) to explain why firing him would destroy the company. (Grandiosity: Not a word in this guy's vocabulary.) Another became catatonic. She just sat there and refused to answer, staring into space for ten minutes—which was so frightening, Donna called EMS, thinking the woman might be having a stroke. At any rate, every firing situation is sad, even if the reason for firing is something criminal, like fraud. It's amazing how little self-awareness even the smartest people can have, how they try to justify their behavior, and often how their behavior when fired—screaming, berating, bullying—is a perfect example of what got them fired in the first place.

As it turns out, having to issue the Donald Trumpish "You're fired" scores of times helped Donna prepare for getting her husband out of the house. Both of us know something most people don't: In addition to the initial upset most people experience, there are a surprising number who send you flowers six months later and say, "Thank you." People become so invested in the way they're behaving, they cannot see another way to approach things until they are forced to do so.

Being fired is generally the last step in a series of strained conversations and failed performance evaluations designed to drive change. By the time you are actually being fired, there is nothing you can do to change it (yelling, begging, phone calls, letters) because the decision has been made. You have to earn your job back by proving that you're worth it. But in certain instances, being fired can be the world's most unpleasant first step toward self-knowledge, and therefore toward happiness.

Essentially, as we said, we were firing our husbands. And they had to work to get their jobs back.

What we did, of course, was extreme, and you might not need to adopt such a radical course. After all, you don't need to kick your husband out if all you're interested in is, say, having him learn how to fill out his own insurance papers.

But the question remains: What are the general principles for making your man more self-sufficient? Here are our basic rules:

No More Enabling: Say you had a colleague or team member at work who wasn't contributing. In the short term, you might work harder to support him, to help him overcome the immediate issues. But in the long term, you have to let someone sink or swim. For those of you who have been micromanaging the details of everyday life, this will be the hardest step. But *this is the rule that makes all other change possible.*

She Who Hesitates . . . Really IS Lost: People hate to change. So once you've determined that making a change is really important, you must take a course of action and stick to it. No going back, no compromise, no "wait and see." You are skydiving, and you have to trust the parachute to open.

Think about an employee at work who isn't performing. In every office, there are yearly goals. If you know that an employee is missing a goal in February, you wouldn't wait until November to say something. By hesitating or waiting you are doing two things wrong: a) The employee has now been doing his work incorrectly for ten months—bad work has become a habit, and may be harder to correct; and b) you aren't giving him a fair chance (or enough time) to correct his mistakes and try to actually achieve success with the desired goal.

Clear the Roadblocks: Having warned against enabling, it is nevertheless true that if your mate has gotten to the point where he's truly incapable of taking care of himself, you're going to have to help him out one last time; in our case, we thought of this as shoving-the-baby-bird-out-of-the-nest-so-he'd-learn-to-fly.

This is not so much enabling as project planning. In order to help anyone accomplish anything that requires more than one step, you need a plan. The plan should take into account what needs to be done, when it needs to be accomplished, and who should be responsible for each task. Depending on the project, the plan may be for one person to accomplish, or it may be for the whole family to participate in. In business, no one is "accidentally successful." No one falls into a well-executed project—it requires planning, as Julie's story about edging Phillip out of the house illustrates.

When we first discussed the idea of Phillip moving out, he put up TONS of roadblocks. "Who's going to take care of the kids after school?" "Who is going to let the dogs out?" "How will you afford it?" The question underlying all the other questions was: "How will you be able to function without me?"

I could have chosen to say: I don't care what you do, I don't care how you do it—OUT. But at first it seemed cruel. After all, I had played a role in infantilizing my husband, and I couldn't just leave him to his own (nonexistent) devices. So initially, I decided I had to remove the roadblocks. For every problem, I came up with a solution. I put an ad in the paper for a nanny to pick up the kids after school and to take care of the dogs. I also offered to let Phillip have the dogs or to get rid of them.

Now I have to admit, this was an idle threat. I had gotten my pugs from a rescue organization, and trust me, dog rescue people are so insanely protective of their charges, there is probably more paperwork to adopt a pug than there is to adopt a human. They pick the kind of people (read: me) who would never abandon a dog. But the very fact that I would make the threat about my fugly little babies rattled Phillip. It meant I was serious.

Once the major obstacles were cleared, I started looking for apartments around our neighborhood that Phillip could afford. Were they as nice as the house he was living in? Of course not. But hey, all growing experiences require a little sacrifice. A guy holing up in a tiny, fetid lair post-divorce: Why, it's practically a rite of passage! So I brought home apartment guides, circled newspaper ads, and told him about signs I'd seen in front of houses saying FOR RENT. *I found an apartment down the street for less than $1,000 a month. At this point, even though his contribution was not huge, Phillip was still paying some of the bills—so I was sacrificing, too. It was a big deal that I would no longer have his income. I might have to give up the cell phone, getting my nails done, the fifty magazine subscriptions, the eating-out-anywhere-but-Denny's. But I didn't care; it would be worth it to regain some semblance of a life.*

Needless to say, Phillip balked at the apartment. There is a rule in Chicago that if you are a cop, you have to live inside city limits. He was trying to become a cop, and we live in the suburbs.

Another roadblock.

And that's when I learned that sometimes you really do have to Just Say No. Or, in this case, OUT. What seemed unthinkable at first became the only chance I had, short of a Taser, of getting him out the door. Finally, I turned to him and said, "It's up to you—I don't care where you move to, but you have to move."

Roadblock #5,575: "I've been giving you most of my paychecks each month. I don't have enough for a deposit."

Solution: "Here's $1,000.00. Buh-bye." (That wasn't exactly the conversation, but close.)

Phillip continued to insist the whole thing was impossible. Finally, I did what perhaps I should have done from the beginning: I got a rental truck and started to sort through our stuff. It was at that point he realized he'd better have a place at the other end of the truck's journey to unload his goods.

As you can imagine, these were not good times. Lots of screaming, lots of furious silence. Each step in inching him out the door was a new fight and a chance to show how truly passive-aggressive he could be. To simply get him to call the utility company and get service—that would be a battle. This is how our conversations would go:

Me: Did you call the cable company?

Phillip: I can't get cable service at the new place.

Me: Why not?

Phillip: Because the cable account here is in my name. I'm not allowed to have two cable accounts.

I got him to call the company and tell them he was moving. But he would not tell them that I wanted a separate cable account. Instead, right before he was supposed to leave:

Phillip: By the way, you'd better call the cable company. They're turning off your cable service tomorrow.

So again, I would have to remove the roadblock—that is, call the cable company and get the account at my house reinstated and put in my name.

As crazy-making as these games were, I knew that once he was gone and set up, that was it: He was on his own. And at least he was being forced, however reluctantly, to participate in the process of becoming an adult again.

Self-sufficiency Begins with the Wallet: For us, as for so many battling couples, the arena of greatest fighting was over money. It's not that we didn't believe child care was a valid contribution— far from it. Child care has a significant financial value, and if our husbands had been taking care of the children, we would never say they weren't really working. We'd do a mental balance sheet in terms of contribution for the service provided against funds coming in from our salaried jobs.

But we also had to admit that the longer our husbands went without bringing in an income themselves, the more they began to treat our incomes as if they were Monopoly money. And worse.

When Donna found out Dave was spending money (HER money) on another woman, she was devastated—even though Dave and this other woman weren't sleeping together. In some ways it was worse: Theirs was a romance that hadn't yet become physical. So he was spending money on *wooing* her. And in the meantime, Donna was strapped for cash to provide things for the family, not understanding where the money was going.

And as Julie explains about her financial tug-of-war:

I have a very detailed system of receipts that I actually look forward to reconciling each month when I get my bank statements. OK, so maybe I'm a little extreme. I am As One with my Excel spreadsheet. I have charts with plans and little boxes I check off as I accomplish things. I often wait until I have the time to enjoy this task; I don't want to rush it and ruin the moment. (Afterward, I have a cigarette. . . .)

Now I don't expect, or indeed want, anyone to be as anal as I am. But Phillip? It wasn't just a question of not keeping careful records. The only filing he ever did was in the garbage can. His solution to many annoying small pieces of paper? Throw them away! Before we were married, he was perfectly capable of balancing a checkbook. Afterward . . . it seemed that his wedding band somehow cut off circulation to the part

*of his brain that involved addition and subtraction. His idea
of checkbook balancing would be to write down a figure—
"June, $512.64"—and then tell me the rest was in his head.*

*Perhaps most frightening was his teenage-boy attitude
toward money: He bought whatever he wanted, whenever he
wanted it. I once found a set of custom golf clubs he'd paid
way too much for hidden in the garage, like a junkie hiding
his stash.*

In both of our situations, the ATM cards were cut up; the
checkbooks were hidden. We assumed almost all of the shared
debt. If our spouses wanted money—any money—they had to
have their own bank accounts and checkbooks. We concen-
trated on getting them to send only certain important change-
of-address notifications (like for payments for Dave's vehicle);
for the most part, we still had joint accounts, but they knew we
were taking over 100 percent of the payments.

Why? Two reasons. 1) You really *can't* get blood from a
stone—they just didn't have money; and 2) after all that bickering and negotiation, we wanted to experience the delicious
freedom of answering to no one but ourselves. We've seen too
many of our women friends go to court over monetary disputes,
expecting their children's fathers to pay part or half, only to
have those expectations not met.

There were, of course, some expenses we didn't worry about
at all. We were lucky to be married to men who could take their
own cars apart and put them back together again, so car mainte-
nance wasn't an issue. And we weren't going to nickel-and-
dime them over things like car insurance. The men were going
out on their own, they had no money, they needed their cars;

and since we feared that they might be boneheaded enough to drop the insurance and ensnare us in some legal problems if they had an accident, well, we coughed up the money ourselves.

But credit cards were different. Credit cards were our battleground—and had been, on occasion, our Waterloo.

Julie and Phillip had a credit card with a large balance that went back to the beginning of their marriage, when they were barely getting by. Her big spender husband continued to use this card, yet Julie never saw a receipt. And she noticed that once she made his ATM card disappear, he would use the credit card for many small purchases every day. If she paid the minimum monthly payment, or she managed to scrape together enough to make a moderate payment, it didn't matter: It felt like throwing a pebble into a lake that somehow caused her to get hit with a tidal wave. Finally, in disgust, she gave up. And at 17 percent interest a year, she really couldn't afford to give up.

When Julie turned Phillip loose with his own checking account and handed the card over to him, he actually started to manage it a little more closely since he was now responsible for the input and the output.

Which makes sense, really. Think about the guy on the factory line at work. He may be screwing one nut into one bolt all day long; if he never sees, or rides in, the glorious BMW he's helped to create, he'll have no curiosity about what went into the making of that vehicle nor pride in his role in putting it together. When we're working with a team of people, we make sure they see the end process of all their efforts.

Not every woman can afford to just let her husband off the hook in this way. But if you can—if you have been paying most of the bills anyway—do it. For now. Here's why: For a man who is even a little motivated to get back to his family, the lack of financial entanglement can be deeply unsettling. It's like playing tug-of-war with a dog. When you're tugging, the dog is growling and desperate to get the rope away from you. When you drop the rope and let him have it, he is immediately bewildered, lost . . . and desperate to get you to tug back.

We dropped the rope.

You Can't Learn Self-confidence with Someone Breathing Down Your Neck: Micromanaging may have short-term benefits, but in the long run you destroy people's confidence. If you constantly correct your staff, you end up with a team of losers—a high price to pay so that *you* can be right.

That means if you want your husband to learn how to use Excel or iron a crease in his own pants, you show him once . . . and back off. If he wants more explanation, he'll ask for it. And if he wants to iron the pants his way, not yours . . . even if the crease isn't as crisp . . . *back off.*

We had to keep this precept in mind, praising our husbands when they did something that may not have been our way of doing it but ultimately still worked out fine for the family.

For example, when our husbands were arranging their new homes, we had to be very careful about when to make demands and when to back off. He wants a fifty-inch plasma TV rather than a dining room table? Fine. *If you can scrape up the money, knock yourself out.* The kids can eat on the floor. (Soon, he'll be buying that dining room table.) But for the children to be happy visiting him they need to keep some of their stuff (books, videos, toys) around. For us, this was nonnegotiable. For a long time, Dave argued that his "crash pad" was not suitable for the kids. Uh, wrong: It's not your crash pad, it's your home, and it's going to be your kids' home, too.

Donna realized Dave was finally taking her seriously when he made the place homey; her decidedly non-metrosexual guy's guy got color-coordinated towels for the bathroom, and he even installed a little table in the kitchen so he and the kids could eat meals together rather than eating off TV trays.

Initially, Phillip's place was only marginally less cluttered than the Collyer brothers'. Julie had to take off her glasses when she visited, because she didn't want to see anything too clearly. But still, Phillip was trying. Soon after moving in to his own place, he discovered baking cookies with the kids. Well, "baking" is a bit of an exaggeration: Basically, Phillip discovered those premade cookie dough cutouts you break apart and shove in the oven. To Julie, those cookies made up for the damp laundry attracting fungus in the corner.

Thinking back on that time now, we are happy we didn't nag our husbands about things like dirty laundry. Because during that time, we both realized how far away *we* were from our fifties-housewife ideal.

So if you are working not on something as huge as having your husband set up a separate household, but something simple—dressing the new baby himself, finding the sugar bowl without having to call you to the kitchen Every. Freaking. Time—let him find his own way of accomplishing that task, no matter how different it may be from yours. Maybe the baby's diaper is on backward and the kid is dressed like P. Diddy; maybe the sugar bowl is in the spot *he* remembers to put it rather than in the perfect place it's always lived. So what? Your goal is not to be right; your goal is to help him rely on you less.

Limit Your Availability: You took every phone call. You listened to every complaint. You were there to solve the problems 24/7.

Now you're not.

When Phillip and Julie broke up, initially she was going to insist Phillip keep a cell phone, and then she thought: What am I doing? Making sure he has a phone so he can contact me the moment something goes wrong?

We've both become convinced that paring down on technology can make a breakup easier. If you're not constantly available to your spouse through cell phone, BlackBerry, or computer (you need your e-mail, but you can at least block his IMs), you will not be subject to the barrage of cries for help.

Pick Your Battles: Did you know that, before we kicked our husbands out of the house, they were superheroes? Yes! Their super-power consisted of creating an invisible force field around any task we required them to do. The socks dropped next to the bed? Couldn't be picked up—invisible force field. The paper towels crumpled and left all over the house? Force field. And a pile of laundry or stack of dishes was protected not only by the force field but a shield that hid those problems from sight. Well, hid them from *their* sight, anyway.

Absolving themselves of the most basic of domestic chores was, they will tell you now, a very real, very male form of revenge.

In this arena of must-be-done household chores, for God's sake pick your battles: This is where our original prioritizing system will be particularly useful. An Oscar is not going to become a Felix; a man who believes a Hot Pocket is a delicious, wholesome meal is not going to become your own personal Jamie Oliver.

Years ago in college, Julie took a class called "Marriage and Family." At one point the professor asked the class, "How many ways are there to clean dishes?" Everyone deliberated for several minutes on the correct answer, with a great deal of discussion about different kinds of soap; rinsing versus not rinsing before putting in the dishwasher, soaking or not soaking, etc., etc.

After this heated debate, the professor interrupted everyone. "There's only one way to clean dishes: They must go from being dirty to clean. Everything else is irrelevant." His point: Many family arguments arise from the discussion about what the right way is between two points such as these instead of agreeing on the end point.

So we had to let go of our way of doing things—THE way, as we thought of it—and just establish the ultimate goal.

It's His Body. Let Him Care for It: If you've spent more than twenty seconds in male company this probably won't come as a shock to you: In general, men are not good patients. They don't take pain or discomfort well, they don't listen to their doctors closely, and they don't *go* to their doctors regularly. In fact, a 2003 study at the University of California, Los Angeles, demonstrated that when given the same pain stimulus, men and women react completely differently. In men, the pain stimulates more of the cognitive part of the brain, triggering a fight-or-flight response. (Translation: They get a cold, and they're either in denial or wallowing in their own misery.) In women, pain triggers the emotional centers of the brain. (Translation: We recognize we don't feel well, which makes us unhappy—and then we do something about it.) Is it any wonder that on average women live four years longer than men—not only in the United States, but in almost every country in the world?

Before we separated from our husbands, any sniffle would

trigger this kind of exchange—generally while both of us were at work, and almost always when we had some sort of deadline.

Phillip: My throat hurts.
Julie: Oh, that's too bad.
Phillip: I think I'm coming down with something.
Julie: Call the doctor.
Phillip: I don't have the number.
Julie: Here's the number.
Phillip: I don't *know* the doctor. You call.
Julie: [Pause. Deep breath.] OK, when are you free?
Phillip: Call and see what appointments are available. Then call me back. I'll tell you if I can make it.

You can probably guess what it took to get our husbands to set up appointments and take the *children* to the doctor. Clearly, this was not going to happen. Our husbands refused to learn the names, addresses, or phone numbers of any medical professionals; apparently, they needed to keep that part of their brains cleared for more important information, like the win/loss history of the Bears versus the Vikings. When they got ill, sometimes we thought *we* would kill them before any virus did them in.

So when we moved out, we gave them a medical "kit": the names and phone numbers of their doctors, the local hospital, the pharmacy, and the children's doctors—plus little MapQuest maps we downloaded from the Internet, telling them how to get there. (Our husbands responded well to any information that came on a map. Your husband may vary.) We also provided them with a packet of information about their benefits and insurance plans—with the number of the insurance provider highlighted in yellow, since we knew beyond a doubt that neither had ever filled out insurance paperwork and would surely need some help.

Once Phillip made his first appointment with our doctor, it was the beginning of a beautiful relationship. She seemed smitten with him. Secretly (OK, not so secretly . . . he gloats), he is pleased that when Julie calls the doctor she gets treated like any patient. (Recently, Julie asked for a referral to a chiropractor; the doctor told her to exercise.) When Phillip calls the response is invariably, "Sure, I can squeeze you in today!"

Keep Your Children in the Loop: Obviously, your children don't need to know about picayune financial or domestic arrangements—that, say, Dad is now going to be responsible for paying half the bills in the house, or that he will now be responsible for bringing his own clothes to the dry cleaner's. But they should be apprised, in a manner appropriate to their age, of changes that affect them. In our case, of course, those changes were huge.

On the days our husbands moved out, we talked to our kids. And talked and talked. We wanted to normalize the event as much as we could, so even though it was real and serious and there was nothing they could do to change it, it would not appear that Dad was driving away from *them* permanently—even though both Donna and I did think divorce was inevitable.

We made the kids active participants in the process. We took them shopping for housewarming items for Dad, for example—a coffeemaker, a Walkman and CDs, some DVDs, video games, books. We didn't want the kids to think that Daddy didn't have what he needed because Mommy had kicked him out or because Mommy was an ogre.

Julie had agreed that the kids would be spending every other weekend with their father, so she had them move some of their own stuff over there—and got them duplicates of a few prized items (hey, if they felt more comfortable visiting Dad because he, too, had a copy of their favorite PlayStation racing game it seemed a small price to pay).

Donna even tried to make Dave's moving-out day like going off to college. Isn't it exciting? Wow, Daddy has a pool! Hey, isn't this TV going to be great for PlayStation? She wanted it to be as "normal" for the kids as it could be, even if she had to manufacture the normalcy.

Her daughter Chelsea, who was about three at the time, asked one night shortly after the move why Daddy had to live in his own "compartment." Ironically, one of the things that made the discussion with the kids easier was the fact that Daddy had been Scary Daddy for quite some time, and they were anxious being around him. So Donna told them directly that Daddy was unhappy, and that part of his unhappiness had to do with Mommy; that she was sorry she did things to make Daddy unhappy, but the things were not things she could change, and that it was her hope that Daddy would find happiness and that would be good for everyone. She wanted him to be kind to the kids, to have fun with him, and there was a chance that things would end up even better and it might be because Mommy and Daddy weren't living together.

Sure, it felt strange, but we didn't want the kids to wake up one morning and find Dad had cleared out his stuff; this has always seemed like an incredibly bad idea. As adults, we'd heard too many stories from friends where they had no idea what was going on and Mom/Dad disappeared while they were at the movies or spending the night with a friend.

We always set up the expectation that it was permanent. The last thing we wanted was for our kids to be sucked into any adult indecision.

Essentially, we utilized the same reasoning a company does in throwing a party for someone who's been let go. Rather than just letting the employee skulk away, when possible it's better to leave the impression that this is an agreeable, if sad, situation for everyone. Certainly this beats the perception that this person has been excised like a tumor from the corporate body.

The Person Who Masters His Anger, Wins: Especially when there are children involved.

Let us explain.

Needless to say, we were both angry—very angry. But there is an old expression that is especially applicable to the business world: "Don't burn your bridges, because you never know when you may need to cross them again."

That puppet-head in publicity you thought you'd never see after you left your job? He's now the director of marketing at your new firm. Your dragon-lady boss who you took a pay cut to escape? OK, now she's not your boss at your new company; she's one of your clients. We're sure this is one of God's little jokes: The more annoying the guy in the cube next to yours at your first job, the greater the chances he will pop up at your retirement party.

So for us, who knew what the future held?

That's why we did everything we could to keep the children from knowing how angry we were. We didn't criticize, we didn't complain. We had already fought in front of them; we wanted them to experience this separation as a cooling-off period for everyone. Our work—coming to a structured environment every day, where we had to hold it together—was a godsend. It didn't allow us the luxury of wallowing, of succumbing to the whole "woe is me, I'll be alone forever" mentality.

We hope that splitting up isn't on the agenda for you. But if it is, and you ignore everything else in this chapter, hear us out on this: Assuming your mate is not abusive or neglectful, helping him to maintain a relationship with his own children is the most important aspect of your separation.

You may think he's a dimwitted lowlife, and maybe he is. But he's the only dimwitted lowlife your children have. Hate him, ignore him, mock him with your friends . . . but to your kids he is still Dad, the Supreme Being. Or put another way: He is the well, and if you poison the well you are poisoning *them.*

So your most important job may be to keep the bonds of father and child together, even if Father is seemingly too addled or lame at this point to do it for himself.

Let Go and Let God: We do not literally mean surrendering yourself to God here. We mean, simply, to understand that not everything is in your control. We talk about "fixing" our marriages as if we were ace mechanics. But one of the toughest parts of getting our marriages back on track was acknowledging that, ultimately, we could not single-handedly be the fixers. Change comes from within, and if we were married to men who fundamentally weren't interested in getting their wives or their kids back, there was nothing we could do about it. BUT: There was a great deal we could do to create the optimal environment and circumstances to motivate them to change. At some point you realize that this is a litmus test, and he either passes or he fails. Either he changes or he doesn't, but you have to be prepared to walk away if he doesn't.

The Serenity Prayer can be very useful to you at this time: *God, grant me the serenity to accept the things I cannot change, courage to change the things I can, and the wisdom to know the difference.*

Don't Forget to Celebrate Even the Baby Steps Forward: For both of us, kicking out our husbands initially meant one thing: We were going to have 100 percent responsibility for everything. But we were going to have 100 percent freedom, too.

This pleasure can't be overstated. Think about it—what had we been doing for years? We were in constant negotiations, and we were *still* paying all the bills. We had to listen to another person's needs, all the while being bitter and resentful and watching our marriages dissolve.

When they left, we paid the bills and did what we pleased. We were responsible for ourselves and our young children, who were not yet self-reliant. Our lives became streamlined. Homework, movies, bedtimes, chores . . . the whole mess of having to discuss life decisions with another individual who brings his values and perspectives to the table: GONE.

Julie distinctly remembers this: The first time she posed the question "What do you want for dinner?" and the subject didn't have to be debated like she was on a segment of *Crossfire* . . . well, that was one of the most satisfying days of her life.

After a few months, the men began to take stock of their own lives. They began to contribute—on their own terms, in their own way. Because we did not expect anything from them, there was no nagging—and they actually had to remember for themselves when there was a bill coming up involving *their* children toward which *they*, as reasonable adults, might be expected to contribute.

For example, Philip's hockey expenses. (Note to our readers: Julie's husband is named Phillip, and Donna's son is Philip—with one "l." We arranged this specifically to confuse you.) At the time Dave was moving out, Philip was in the midst of winter hockey season. The sport is expensive—it costs around $5,000 a year—and the club allows you to split the payment into five equal parts. Donna had made two payments. One day, Dave gave her a check for 2.5 payments—unasked for. She did not know what the money was for until she asked him. He had called the hockey club to find out how much the total was for the season, and the check was payment for half. Dave began to make it his business to check on expenses like this regularly. It was shocking, sort of like having your sullen fifteen-year-old ask you not only if he could go to church, but whether you wanted him to wear his khaki suit or his seersucker.

When our husbands began to follow through on these first basic steps for living, we felt a surge of hope. But remember: There were *two* people who needed to change here. Refraining from trying to manage the situation was a huge step for us. It took every ounce of self-control not to become Miss Debbie Follow-Through, micromanaging and evaluating our husband's progress from Step A to Step Z. As managers, we find it difficult to pull back and delegate tasks to a trainee, when we know the work would be done more quickly (and often better) by ourselves. I often think of this problem when it comes to training not just someone in a corporate environment but in a situation where training and repetition genuinely make a difference between life and death. Remember: As terrifying as it must be for the people in charge of training him, a rookie cop always has to go into his first gunfight, a resident surgeon always has to make her first incision.

Life and death. Well, getting our husbands to take care of themselves represented the life or death of our marriages.

CHAPTER 3

Work

Become Productive

• • • • •

Life is a progress, and not a station.

—RALPH WALDO EMERSON

What do women need to succeed? No, breast implants and in-difference to toxic male behavior are not the right answers. (Well, not always.) According to a 2001 study at the University of Alabama at Birmingham, the common denominator of fe-male success is education and a stable home life. Apparently, men can be feral and still be CEOs of Fortune 500 companies. Women, on the other hand, need to know everything is running smoothly at home—that the kids are doing their homework and the husband isn't spending every waking moment surfing Web sites of women named Misty—before she can go out and con-quer the world.

What this means, practically, is that it's not enough for us to be productive. In order for us to succeed, we need our husbands to be productive, too. It doesn't matter what form their pro-ductivity takes—whether they're heads of the PTA or General

Motors. The important thing is that they are happy and engaged in what they're doing every day, which will allow them to be supportive of *us*.

OUR SCORECARD FOR PRODUCTIVITY

···

- **Identify your interests**
- **Pick your career**
- **Develop a plan for working toward immediate career goals**
- **Prepare and send out resume; job hunt**
- **Reach out to resources (friends, classified ads, employment agencies, etc.)**
- **Study, train, and test for requirements**
- **Obtain necessary certification**
- **Become employed**
- **Earn enough money to support your desired lifestyle**
- **Further your progress with long-term career goals**

···

✳ "Whistle While You Work": ✳
Your Scorecard for Productivity

STEP ONE—Prioritize: List all the ways you'd like your husband to be more productive. Fill them in on their proper place on your four-block chart, identifying which items are of highest priority for you. Our Work Chart looked like this:

✶ OUR RELATIONSHIP MAP: PRODUCTIVITY ✶

ND	**ID**
• Prepare and send out resume • Reach out to resources (friends, classified ads, employment agencies, etc.) • Job hunt • Further your progress with long-term career goals	• Evaluate your interests • Identify your dream • Pick your career • Develop a plan for working toward career goals • Become employed • Earn enough money to support your desired lifestyle
NS	**IS**
	• Study, train, and test for requirements • Obtain necessary certification

LEVEL OF DISSATISFACTION

IMPORTANCE

STEP TWO—Filter: Take the items in the upper right quadrant of your four-block—the items of highest importance and greatest dissatisfaction.

For each item, ask:

Can I fix this myself? (And if the answer is yes):

- Is there a one-time fix to this issue? (That is, he seems unable to produce a good-looking resume, but I'm better at setting things up on the computer, so this is really no big deal.)
- Can I fix this with technology or a new product that is on the market? (For instance, my husband did his resume, but a college student/entrepreneur is making

money editing them and mailing them out. Might as well hire him.)

These are the items you can handle. Set them aside. For all others in the upper right-hand quadrant, continue to step three.

STEP THREE—Analyze: For items that remain, you'll need to develop an approach to fixing them. Determine whether an item is going to be easy or hard to fix by asking yourself the following questions:

- Is my husband going to be cooperative on this issue? (There are some issues that might be solved by a well-planned conversation, but others where you know that your partner will be entrenched in his point of view, custom, or cultural perspective.)
- Do we (my husband or I) have the skills necessary to properly address this issue?
- Has this been an issue for less than one year?
- Can the task be done by only one person?

If you answered "yes" to all of these—we would call your problem easy. If you answered "no" to any of the questions—your problem would be considered hard.

For Easy Problems: We recommend approaching your husband with a recommendation and a quick conversation. Perhaps you suggest he go to a career counselor, seminar, or networking event.

For Hard Problems: We recommend that if your husband isn't cooperative, prep work may be needed in order to gain agreement or compliance. If neither of you has the skill set, you may need to go to training or pay someone else to do it (counseling, career planning, etc.).

STEP FOUR—Plan Your Approach: With Phillip, Julie did what in business is called the "blue sky/green field exercise": In other words, if the sky's the limit, and there are no impediments, what would you want to do? In this exercise, you start with the dream and work backward to see how you can fulfill it. This approach was critical to Phillip, who knew what he wanted—to be a cop—but always had some reason why he couldn't do it: the commute into the inner city would be too long, he wouldn't pass the physical, he'd have to give too long a notice on his current job, etc. The trick was to make the dream not overwhelming, but something that could be accomplished in incremental steps. Phillip couldn't quite start the process on his own. But once he saw how Julie created a "recipe" of steps toward his goal, he could, in fact, take the (proverbial) ball and run with it.

> **CORE STRATEGIES FOR SUCCESS:**
> **Time Management**
> **Resource Management**

We loved thinking our husbands would feel fulfilled being at home with the children. And there are men who feel this way. Unfortunately, we were not married to them. Because most American men's identities are wrapped up in their work, a man who isn't working outside the home, we have found, is one who is sullen, anxious (one in seven men who lose their jobs become clinically depressed), restless—and often competitive with us. Talk about a recipe for marital disaster.

We'd like to think we've come a long way, baby. And in many

ways we have. But those of us in the second wave of feminism—where we take for granted our right to a career and wages equal to any man's—have blinded ourselves to one fact of human nature: For most men, not working is emasculating. There, we said it. The PC police can arrest us.

Our problem happened to be husbands who were not working—or barely working—at all. For many more women, the problem is more subtle. Their husbands have careers; they have good incomes. What these men may not have is any sense of satisfaction or happiness. Americans are working longer and longer hours to support diminishing lifestyles. The eager law student has turned into the eighty-hour-work-week corporate drone who never sees his wife and children. The marketing whiz becomes disillusioned when he realizes that maybe pushing Red Bull on twelve-year-olds isn't a goal to aspire to. We have been raised to believe work should bring to our lives not only money but meaning. Some men can do without the meaning part of the equation very well. For others, life without meaningful work is hollow.

If living with a thirty-five-year-old in full-blown career crisis isn't bad enough, many of us are living with men who, through no fault of their own, have been laid off or are underemployed due to a highly competitive job market or a lack of current skills. There is a whole generation of men who came of age in the eighties and early nineties and went into then-booming fields, like technology and advertising; they thought the gravy train would never end. Imagine their surprise to discover that whole sectors of the job market were virtually wiped out within a few years.

Our point is this: You don't have to be living with a man who's totally unemployed to know how devastating, and para-

lyzing, career problems can be. And we tend to listen, to sym-
pathize endlessly—and watch our husbands do nothing. *If you're
not going to do anything about your situation, shut up already!* we
think. But we keep listening, keep advising . . . and watch with
sadness and fury as our men flounder.

When Donna fell in love with Dave, she wanted a father for her
children, not a Master of the Universe. Dave had never known
his biological father; he came from the kind of rural family that
shot its own food. Donna, on the other hand, grew up in a posh
suburb with an ambitious, hardworking father, regular vacations to cool places, and yearly tickets to the *Radio City Christmas Spectacular*. She adored her dad but rarely saw him. Money
is great, but having a dad around, she felt, was greater. So the
fact that Dave wasn't wildly ambitious in the corporate sense—
the fact that he'd be more of a clock-in, clock-out worker—was
fine because it would allow him to spend the kind of quality time
with his family that Donna felt was important. Dave is great at
sports and Donna envisioned him at home in the early evening,
teaching their children to play ball, coaching their sports teams
on weekends, and being at home rather than traveling.

The operative word, though, is *worker*. Donna was not prepared for someone who did not know what he wanted to do at
all, and at various points seemed not to care. They spent so
much time discussing his career that at some stages she felt like
a living, breathing, jabbering volume of *What Color Is Your Parachute?* But Donna was not so perfect, either. As she recalls:

*Now here, I have to admit something. The fabulous career
woman you see before you today started out with one lofty*

goal: to have a really good time. I had a really great party when I graduated college, and I managed to extend that party for a good five years. I took a series of administrative positions that worked around my real job of barhopping and meeting men. School had always been easy for me; I was on scholarship and maintained great grades. I thought about becoming a lawyer (Dave will attest to my love of winning arguments), but after interning at a corporate law division of a Fortune 500 company, I thought: Too hard. I thought I might teach, maybe write . . . I had visions of writing for Rolling Stone, *though for all the wrong reasons. . . .*

In addition to not being very career-oriented at the time, Donna met Dave after having been through several unsatisfactory relationships that had her trying to morph into whatever the man-of the-moment wanted. Like so many of us, she suffered from that lack of confidence that prevented her from finding balance in love: Either she loved the guy and the love was unrequited or vice versa.

Part of Donna's healing process was to actively look for someone who was the polar opposite of the others. Whereas she generally preferred pretty boys, this time she sought out ruggedness. Where she typically hooked up with self-centered idiots, she looked for a man who made her the center of his universe. And where she had sought brainiac sparring partners, she now looked for someone who found pleasure in the physical rather than the intellectual. She also consciously looked for a counterbalance to her own slightly neurotic, high-maintenance self.

So when Donna met Dave, who was romantic and caring and adored her, it was easy to fall in love with him. Everybody loves

Dave. He's funny, sweet, and good at just about every game and sport that exists. And he's extremely easygoing—a very nice counterbalance to Donna herself.

Dave was in the navy when they met, and stayed there almost until their marriage. Donna had moved back to Connecticut from California and got a position at GE, which eventually put her on the path she's on now. By 1992, she had gotten serious. She cleaned up her act and started thinking in terms of a career, not just a job.

When Dave bounced from job to job, Donna told herself that having a husband who was romantic and impulsive beat having a staid, bring-home-the-bacon guy. And for a while it was: When they moved to Chicago from Greenwhich, Connecticut, and Donna's job became more demanding, Dave seemed happy as a stay-at-home dad. Until, that is, he began to act like a sit-com housewife: moping around the house and porking up on bonbons (well, in his case, beer and pork rinds). The dishes were teetering in the sink and the kids were zoning out in front of their PlayStations. Donna didn't want she and Dave to turn into the corporate power couple, but she didn't want them to become directionless couch potatoes, either.

When Julie met Phillip (he answered an ad she placed in the personals, and she fell in love with the sound of his voice on the phone) *he* was the responsible one. Phillip was in the Marines, progressing quickly through the ranks. Julie thought of him as her rescuer, her knight in shining armor: He was going to take care of her and her daughter, Lauren.

Everything changed when Julie earned her undergraduate degree and Phillip got out of the military so they could do something new. Phillip wasn't so sure that the military was for him long-term and didn't want the family to have to continually relocate—which a life in the military would ensure. The plan was for Phillip to become a cop somewhere in the Southeast, such as Georgia, the Carolinas, or even in the Mid-Atlantic region. The couple felt comfortable that Julie would be able to work wherever they moved. The problem? It was harder for him to become a cop than they thought, and it felt like they were running out of time. Julie was graduating in December of 1997 with her undergraduate degree; Phillip had already left the military and had been applying for jobs all over the country. Nothing was happening, and there weren't any jobs where they were. So they changed plans temporarily. Julie would continue to work while getting her MBA and living close to Phillip's family in New Jersey, and Phillip would have more time for job hunting. Julie never dreamed that the temporary change in plans would have resulted in her becoming the primary bread-winner and Phillip taking another five years to find the job he wanted.

For years, Phillip didn't have one clear goal in mind. He buzzed from idea to idea like a bee among flowers. He wanted a career and instead he had a job—or, really, many jobs, all of them dead-end. He was always talking about becoming a cop. But to Julie's never-ending frustration, there was no linkage between the smaller decisions he was making and his progression toward this goal. To Julie, it seemed that if you wanted to be a cop, you would work in fields that were similar, such as security, to be around people you could network with. Worst-case scenario: Volunteer to get close to it. Phillip was getting frustrated because, unless you know someone, it's difficult and time-consuming to get into the field. What Julie and Phillip didn't understand at the time was that many areas of the country only hire cops with past experience because they can't afford to do the training themselves.

Today, Julie admits that some of her dissatisfaction with her husband's role stemmed from dissatisfaction with her own. She had visions of Phillip being the breadwinner while she was the supportive stay-at-home wife taking care of the kids—or perhaps she would work part-time in a small company. She had never had the opportunity to stay home with their children and assumed she would like it when the roles were reversed. Maybe it was old-fashioned, but what Julie wanted most was to be a wife and mother; she had never planned on being the primary breadwinner in the family. Why did Phillip have the luxury of choosing his path while she couldn't pursue hers? (In years since, Julie has acknowledged she wouldn't have been happy staying at home. But she still daydreams about winning the lottery and trying it out for fun.) Looking back, Julie sees how she may have inadvertently contributed to Phillip's indecision:

Any time Phillip got excited about something, I would get doubly excited, then research it and talk about it incessantly until he never, ever wanted to think about it again. I would check out ads in the newspaper, look at Web sites for him, make contacts ("Honey, my friend at work has a cousin/ brother/neighbor who works at the police department—let's get together with them and talk about it"), update his resume, make thousands of suggestions. Some of this was for Phillip, but much of it was for me. For example, at one point Phillip mentioned he wanted to be a helicopter pilot. Whoopee, a goal! I got a loan, found a place for him to take a class, and gave him a check. He did get his license—but then . . .

nothing. Sure, there are probably police officers who combine their work with flying helicopters, but it's not like there are tons of spots available for pilot/cops. (Probably he would have been better off taking horseback riding lessons; at least those guys get to march in parades.) I was constantly frustrated by his lack of focus and lack of commitment to what he wanted. But I was also resentful because I felt as long as he wasn't sure what he wanted to do, I was stuck doing whatever was necessary to pay the bills. He was allowed to pursue his dreams, I wasn't—and yet he was the one who was unhappy.

I wanted Phillip to be a guy with a dream. He wasn't. And undoubtedly, he wanted me to stop acting like a mother who, when her child sits down and plinks out "Twinkle, Twinkle, Little Star" on the piano, tries to get him into a master class with Billy Joel.

The turning point for us was when we stopped approaching our husbands like kids, taking every momentary impulse they had as a cue to plan the rest of their lives for them. With their job issues, as with many other problems, we had to learn the fine art of backing off. The truth is, men like to ask for help about as much as they like to ask for directions. We know this. But if they don't ask, at least a little, they are not receptive to receiving. In fact, they will resent you. They will shut down. This is what women don't understand.

We found the following rules indispensable for making our men more productive:

Turn Off the Spotlight: At a certain point we were like little kids in a darkened classroom with laser pointers, constantly bouncing them off the teacher's (i.e., our husbands') faces. We appeared

to be turning the attention on them, but in reality we were trying to get attention ourselves. *Didn't they realize how angry we
were?* (Many women to do this. When we repeatedly ask, "What
are you thinking?" what we really mean is, "Are you thinking
about us?")

So we had to learn to back off until they came to us. This took
months of living on their own. When they finally did ask, we
asked them to approach the problem more systematically, evaluating interests and skill sets, and working toward a goal. Here
are some of the strategies that worked for us:

**Get Your Husband to Do One Thing a Day That Gives Him a Sense of
Accomplishment (and Then Praise Him to the Skies for Doing It):**
Uselessness breeds more uselessness, which in turn breeds depression. If your husband feels unfulfilled at work, or unfulfilled because he has no work, harping on this situation will
only compound the problem. Instead, try to find one thing a day
he can do, or that he's good at, which gives him satisfaction.
Maybe it's painting the garage door. Maybe it's reading your
seven-year-old a chapter of *Harry Potter*. Maybe it's simply
something like taking a run—and he's more likely to do it if you
go with him. (Hey, a win/win situation!). Whatever it is, focus on
finding *one* thing a day . . . and give him props for it. We truly
believe that when a man is in a rut with work, he's forgotten what
it is to be pleased with himself, and even minor accomplish-
ments can remind him. But whatever that accomplishment is, it
doesn't have to be career- or job-related. From our experience,
pride in one arena of life seeps over into pride in others.

Offer (Limited) Help Only When It's Requested: We have friends who
have fraternal twin boys. One, Henry, was big and boisterous;

the other, Gus, was tiny, gentle, and a bit klutzy. Henry's first sentence was "I do it myself!" Gus's first sentence was "Pick me up, please!" Of course, the parents felt tenderly toward Gus, who seemed so much more helpless. So they were always stepping in to help him, always, even when he stopped asking for help.

You can pretty much guess which twin was the first to walk, dress himself, use the potty, fetch the mail, and start to read. They are now four, and Gus still needs assistance with everything from walking down the street (he still likes to be carried) to eating (if someone is there to feed him, he'll pretend he doesn't have arms). His parents have finally realized that helping is *not* helping in the long term.

It's not so different with grown men. We both had to learn to limit our help to when it was specifically requested.

One day, Julie just asked Phillip, "If you could do anything, what would it be?" Until that day, he seemed unable to put a name on what he wanted; he would say, vaguely, "I want a promotion at my current job," "I want more money," or "I want to be a helicopter pilot." Perhaps he was frightened he wasn't capable of doing what he really wanted to do. But that day, he said it, finally: He wanted to be a cop. His decision was unequivocal. Only then could he really start the process of making his dream come true.

But at the same time, Julie had to stop asking Phillip questions about his process—and when she did ask, she was careful about the language she used. If she asked him whether he'd been "networking" with people about what it was like being a cop in Chicago, he'd change the subject. The language just reminded Phillip that he was out of the mainstream, a pariah among his friends. So networking became, "Have you talked to friends?"

Even after Phillip finally made up his mind, it took two years for him to get a job on the police force—but Julie came to realize that this was truly not his fault. It was a disorganized process, and spots had to open up in the area they now lived. Was she desperate to push him to be more aggressive? Yes. Did she push him? No. Because where had the nagging gotten her in the past?

Take Stock of Your Own Expectations: At the end of the day, the only way to set your husband on the road to being a more productive, engaged person is to first look inward and be brutally honest with yourself about what you need from him. If you married a working-class guy who's perfectly happy living paycheck-to-paycheck, and you want the BMW and the month-rental in Tuscany, well, *you've* got the problem: He is productive, but he's not your brand of productive, so there may be the need for you to adjust your expectations. For us, we were not trying to scrub the blue out of our blue-collar guys; although Julie fantasized about not working, she also realized that this was *not* foundational to her happiness.

However, we both finally admitted to ourselves that having our husbands work at something they enjoyed, whatever it was, *was* a deal breaker for us. That was our line in the sand.

Donna's line was that Dave was not going to move back into the house until he had a job he enjoyed and kept, because she was convinced he would become more fulfilled, which would make him happier, and she reasoned that a happier, fulfilled guy would want to find happiness and fulfillment in the other aspects of his life as well. This didn't change the fact that Dave is and always will be Paycheck Guy, not Career Man. (His only criteria for employment are that he not be chained to a desk and that he be outdoors if possible. He would be a forest ranger if they lived, say, near a forest.) And Donna is fine with that. She aspires to nice things but not extravagance, and is perfectly happy to be making more than 50 percent of the income.

Even today, when Dave is working happily as a truck driver, he still struggles with his ability to live within his means. That phrase "generous to a fault" is the dictionary definition of Dave: If he has a dollar, he doesn't see the problem with spending $1.50 and putting the fifty cents on a credit card. It's very hard to yell at someone who spends like this, when he spends it on *you*. (Not that Dave wasn't exceptionally good at spending on himself, as well.) As improved as Dave is, Donna still gets jittery around the holidays.

The big moment of triumph for us came when we realized it was Monday morning, and both our husbands were not clinging to their beds like limpets, dreading the beginning of the week. Dave had to get a truck driver's license in order to be hired permanently for the job he wanted—and still has. This is a rigorous process of training; many fail it the first time, but Dave studied hard and passed it with a very high score. Phillip is a patrolman who loves his work, and, let's face it, is much more at ease wielding a gun than packing school lunches.

To this day, our husbands are still not entirely comfortable with the idea that their wives make more money than they do. But they have learned the lesson that their worth in the marriage is not about the amount on the paycheck at the end of the week.

We do not live rich, but we live well. Our husbands have finally taken to heart the advice of the perpetually-in-debt Mr.
Micawber in *David Copperfield*, who gave young David the following shrewd advice: "Annual income twenty pounds, annual
expenditure nineteen six, result happiness. Annual income
twenty pounds, annual expenditure twenty pounds ought and
six, result misery."

Positive cash flow equals happiness.

CHAPTER 4

Love

Become an Involved Father

• • • • •

I cannot think of any need in childhood as strong
as the need for a father's protection.

—SIGMUND FREUD

In 1992, Nora Ephron wrote and directed a witty, arch movie on
parenthood called *This Is Your Life*, about a frustrated single
mother of two young girls who finds happiness. At one point the
mother, Dottie, gives a speech every mom in the world recog-
nizes. Dottie feels guilty about traveling somewhere for her new
job, and her friend says, "You had to travel. It's part of your
work. Look, kids are happy when their mother is happy." And
Dottie replies, "No, they're not. Everybody says that but it's not
true. Kids are happy if you're there. You give kids a choice, your
mother in the next room on the verge of suicide versus your
mother in Hawaii in ecstasy and they choose suicide in the next
room, believe me."

And this is the truth—kids want their parents to live together, regardless of whether they're happy together. So if we

had told ourselves we would be leaving our husbands—our children's fathers—because we would be happier and therefore our children would be happier, we would have started off our separations with a pleasant lie.

One of the golden rules about fixing a marriage: Don't lie to yourself. About anything.

Fortunately, most of you won't be doing anything as drastic as we did. But many of you would still love to have your husbands more involved with your children. When we talk to our friends, we are always surprised to discover how many fathers—often very loving men—nevertheless know very little about their children's lives. Wouldn't it be wonderful if your husband knew the names of your kids' teachers, had some clue what classes they are taking or what musicals they're performing in or whether they prefer their pizza with pepperoni or just plain cheese?

OUR SCORECARD FOR FATHERING

- Talk to your children individually at least once a day
- Keep track of what they're doing, thinking, and feeling
- Play with kids every day
- Read to kids every night
- Take kids to the park
- Go on bike rides with kids
- Go to movies and on other family outings
- Teach each kid a sport
- Tell children about yourself and what you did at their age
- Treat the kids equally
- Attend recitals, sports, performances, and other events

- Attend parent–teacher conferences
- Review daily homework
- Monitor and support homework plan
- Fill out school paperwork
- Review report cards
- Make school lunches
- Share school drop-off and pickup
- Schedule children's playdates
- Schedule and take kids to appointments
- Share appointment follow-up (pick up prescriptions, schedule next visit, etc.)
- Shop for kids' clothes
- Schedule kids' haircuts
- Monitor kids' chores
- Pay allowance
- Help arrange child care
- Help to arrange after-school schedule, sports, and lessons
- Take kids to parties and other engagements
- Volunteer at school when required

....

✳ "Daddy Dearest": ✳
Your Scorecard

STEP ONE—Prioritize: List all the ways you'd like your husband to be an involved, loving father. Fill them in on their proper places on your four-block chart, identifying which items are of highest priority for you. This is what our Relationship Map looked like:

OUR RELATIONSHIP MAP: FATHERING	

ND	**ID**
• Attend recitals, sports events, performances, etc.	• Talk to your children individually at least once a day
• Attend school events for kids	• Keep track of what they're doing, thinking, and feeling
• Attend parent–teacher conferences	• Play with kids every day
• Review daily homework	• Read to kids every night
• Monitor and support homework	• Take kids to the park
• Fill out school paperwork	• Treat the kids equally
• Review report cards	• Make school lunches
• Shop for kids' clothes	• Share school drop-off and pickup
• Shop for kids' shoes	• Schedule children's play dates
• Schedule kids' haircuts	• Schedule doctor appointments
• Monitor kids' chores	• Schedule dentist appointments
• Pay allowance	

NS	**IS**
• Go on bike rides with kids	• Take kids to appointments
• Go to movies and on other family outings	• Share appointment follow-up (pick up prescriptions, schedule next visit, etc.)
• Teach each kid a sport	• Help arrange child care
• Tell children about yourself and what you did at their age	

(Left vertical axis: LEVEL OF DISSATISFACTION)

IMPORTANCE

STEP TWO—**Filter:** Take the items in the upper right quadrant of your four-block—the items of highest importance and greatest dissatisfaction.

For each item, ask:

- Is there a one-time fix to this issue? For example, under the item "fill out school paperwork," we

all know that school registration is the biggest
single paper chase of the year. Could your husband
be responsible for this and then be done till
next year?

- Can I fix this with technology or a new product that
is on the market? Three of the reasons your husband
hates shopping for the kids' clothes are 1) too much
choice; 2) too much expense; and 3) kids tagging along,
lobbying for crap you don't want to buy them.
Introduce him to online shopping at budget children's
sites like www.kidsurplus.com where kids' clothing is
cheap, choices are manageable, and, best of all, you can
buy without having to drag the kids along. (This works
best for the littler ones. By the time they're in middle
school, all bets are off.)

These are the items you can handle. Set them aside. For all
others in the upper right-hand quadrant, continue to step three.

STEP THREE—Analyze: For items that remain, you'll need to develop an approach to fixing them. Determine whether an item is
going to be easy or hard to fix by asking yourself the following
questions:

- Is my husband going to be cooperative on this issue?
(There are some issues that might be solved by a well-
planned conversation, but others where you know that
your partner will be entrenched in his point of view,
custom, or cultural perspective.)
- Do we (my husband or I) have the skills necessary to
properly address this issue?

- Has this been an issue for less than one year?
- Can the task be done by only one person?

If you answered "yes" to all of these—we would call your problem easy. If you answered "no" to any of the questions—your problem would be considered hard.

For Easy Problems: We recommend approaching your husband with a recommendation and a quick conversation. He may want to spend time teaching your child a sport, but worry a little about a) his level of patience and b) his own competence in that arena. He may just need some reassurance.

For Hard Problems: We recommend that if your husband isn't cooperative, prep work may be needed in order to gain agreement or compliance. If neither of you has the skill set, you may need to find a sports-minded pal or get a coach.

STEP FOUR—Plan Your Approach: When Donna wanted Dave to be more involved in her children's lives, she couldn't just nag in a general way; instead, she had to "edit" his list of choices, and identify the events that would play to his strengths. It was all very well to think that he should be supervising the library book sale or attending the PTA meetings, but the reality was, he would be resentful. So she got him to do what he knew: coach sports teams. First, though, she had to identify and help him overcome certain fears—fears about his own talent, fears that he would be spending most of his time not teaching little kids, but refereeing between crazy, competitive parents. (She had to promise that if the parent politics became too onerous, he could resign from the coaching. Luckily, they didn't.)

CORE STRATEGIES FOR SUCCESS:
Contingency Planning
Prioritizing
Supporting Without Stifling

Almost 25 percent of children in this country grow up without fathers at home. So is it any wonder that many men have never learned how to be dads themselves? There are many permutations of the traditional family where kids can be raised and nurtured wonderfully. But there's still no substitute for a caring dad. (Studies suggest fathers even play differently than mothers do. Perhaps to compensate for the fact that they usually spend less time with their kids than mothers do, dads are often more spontaneous, unpredictable, and, well, fun.)

You're never going to turn someone who is totally uninterested in fathering into a model dad. But don't assume that a man who *was* an interested, loving father can't become one again—and don't assume that the guy who seems indifferent to his three-month-old will be the same kind of father when the child reaches three years. While most women feel that giddy love for a baby right from the beginning (many of our girlfriends compare it to those first few months of being in a new romance), men are not addled by the same hormones we are. To them, a baby is a tiny, smelly intrusion—and not much of a conversationalist.

When Julie met and married Phillip, then a twenty-four-year-old Marine, she was a recently divorced single mother. Phillip was responsible, good-looking, and well mannered. It was easy to fall in love with him, but one of the biggest reasons Julie was dazzled was because he fell in love with her daughter as well.

And when the couple had a child of their own a little earlier than expected, Phillip was a thoughtful, loving man. He even went through a period when he thought he wanted to be a stay-at-home father. He took months off while he was in the military to spend time with their first child together. Julie still remembers coming home from work and finding Phil, beads of sweat dripping off his brow, boiling four pans of water for the baby's bottle nipples.

But then there came the years of career indecision, withdrawal, lack of focus on the family—and a retreat from anything that might be called parenthood. Woody Allen was a more active, involved parent to Mia's children than Phillip was to his and Julie's—and we all know how well that turned out. There was a time when Julie thought of Phillip not as a dad but as a babysitter. For years he was self-involved and self-loathing. And the truth is, how can you care about your children when you don't care about yourself?

Before Phil moved out of the house, he may have loved his children in an abstract way, but they were also a constant distraction from his first loves: television and a six-pack.

Dave's devolution from loving father to non-father was also gradual and devastating. As he became more depressed, he disengaged. He was like a robot living in the house, occasionally barking orders and demands but somehow taking nothing in. Donna's kids wondered why Daddy was always so angry, why he yelled at them all of the time, why he didn't want to do anything with them anymore. This was quite a departure from the summer before when they were out riding bikes every day, going fishing and blackberry picking.

As Dave became more withdrawn, he let the TV become the children's babysitter during the day. Their son, Philip, would come home and do his homework alone. Chelsea had finally gotten to the stage where she was interested in doing something with books other than eating them; this was the prime time to teach her letters and read to her. Instead, Dave slept most of the morning, then flipped on the TV when he got up. Instead of hearing *Goodnight Moon,* Donna walked in one evening to find her three-year-old watching *Reservoir Dogs* on HBO. There were no after-school activities, no sports. One day, Donna asked Dave the name of his children's doctor. He hadn't a clue.

Chelsea was only three and a half when Dave moved out; she was very sad he wasn't living with them but couldn't understand what was going on. She was also a naturally sunny, upbeat little person; when Donna couldn't trust Dave to watch Chelsea all day, she put her in full-time day care, and she adjusted beautifully. But Chelsea still talked about her dad all the time.

Philip, on the other hand, was almost eight and aware of everything. While warm and funny and a wonderful student, he was also by nature a worrier who took other people's problems to heart. During this time he was in a lot of pain. *Daddy's angry . . . what did I do? Why is he always yelling at us?* Dave and Donna didn't fight in a *Who's-Afraid-of-Virginia-Woolf?* way, but Philip was still very scared at the changes in his father. Donna talked to him about his fears. She tried to be very open with him about some of the problems—Dad was not himself, he couldn't be a great dad right now—while still keeping the explanation as simple and unthreatening as possible. Donna said it was likely they would be living without Dave permanently, but that he would still be their dad and Philip would see him all the time. Dave would always be part of Philip's life.

In truth, the kids were used to coming to Donna for most of their needs anyway; they knew she handled all the logistics, all the planning. So from a practical viewpoint there wasn't such a big transition.

By the time Dave moved out, Philip (Donna's son) was relieved, albeit sad and concerned. Donna told him: Sometimes you can love and hate the same person at the same time. Donna talked to her boy about personal responsibility and said that his father had to figure out what he wanted in his life and make some changes.

Our husbands were literally absent from the house, but yours doesn't have to be; we know that a father who's emotionally absent and detached can also cause a child pain. So how did we help our husbands find joy and purpose in the role of fatherhood again? We implemented a few key policies—and stuck to them.

Never Dis Dad: Believe me, we know how hard this is. But both of us, while in pain ourselves, were hell-bent on not exacerbating the pain of our children by ragging on their fathers.

Never Limit Access: One of the smartest things we did was this: While making certain that other aspects of our husbands' lives were harder—their access to our money, for example—we made sure that during our separation, access to their children was easy. We have seen what happens with our friends when a marriage goes south: Hurt spouses want their children on their side, and the kids become pawns in an elaborate and ugly game called Who Do You Love Best? In the end both parents lose, because no child wants to be forced to side with one parent or another, and they will eventually resent even the parent they're loyal to.

Even with a normal situation where Dad's living at home, women sometimes have a way of inadvertently putting themselves between a father and his children (by not approving of the kinds of activities he chooses to do with them, for example). We decided that any kind of father/kid activity, at any time that suited them both, was better than none at all.

After Dave moved out of Donna's home, he would come over in the mornings to have breakfast with his kids. Dave would pick them up from after-school care as much as he could, take them to play at the pool in his apartment complex, and come over to the house for dinner and on weekends. This was actually a struggle for Donna, because while she didn't want to limit Dave's access, she didn't want him to be around her all the time—so she had to find other things to do. As tough as it was, they both benefited: Dave got undivided, unmonitored time with his children, and Donna got off her butt more and went to the gym or spent time with girlfriends. A win/win situation, really. And they both made an effort to attend school events together, to make things as normal for the children as possible.

Don't Assume Your Way of Spending Time with the Children Is THE Way of Spending Time with the Children: When Phillip moved out, he began to do his kinds of things with the kids. This is key. Because in the past, Julie had always defined his desire to be with them based on the kinds of activities she arranged—things like shopping, going to art festivals, visiting bookstores—exactly what *she* enjoyed doing with them.

When Julie stepped back and didn't micromanage their time together, Phillip and the kids did precisely the kinds of things that would have bored Julie to tears: play basketball, throw spirals (which involves tossing a football back and forth ad nauseaum), go biking, etc. The kids were thrilled and constantly wanting to show off some newfound skill. The upshot was that Julie's children would rather play basketball with Dad than go antiquing with her. But that's OK. They've got an entire lifetime to develop adult interests—but they have only one time to be kids with their dad.

Eliminate the Middleman—You. Fathers need their own relationship with their children. Are you helping or hindering that relationship?

When Julie finally kicked Phillip out . . . well, it reminded her of that Joni Mitchell song, "Big Yellow Taxi," with the refrain: "Don't it always seem to go/That you don't know what you got till it's gone? . . ." First, he started sending the girls cards—for every reason and no reason: "Happy Halloween," "Happy Presidents' Day," whatever. They probably got a card a week. And Phillip would call and ask to speak to the kids, then ask them if they got the card and what they thought about it.

It was his first attempt to communicate with them by himself—without Julie moderating or cushioning anything. In the past she'd been so worried about him inadvertently hurting or disappointing them, she'd become his "translator"—constantly butting in, rephrasing what he said, adding her own thoughts, and buffering his. He had a hard time saying what he wanted to say with Julie constantly interrupting with, "What your father means is . . ."

At the time, Julie thought she was helping. Many of us do. In truth, all our "translating" makes the problem worse.

Once we stopped acting as translators, our husbands began

to truly talk to their children again—without fear of us jumping down their throats. Instead of just barking orders, our husbands began explaining what they wanted from the kids, and why. Not that you ever have to justify to a child why you are asking her to do something but she's more likely to comply (and not be told the same thing 500 times) if she understands the reason behind the request. If Phillip wanted his daughter to help with the laundry, for example, he would take the time to explain why you use hot water for whites, or why putting laundry away as soon as it comes out of the dryer would save it from becoming too wrinkled. And both Phillip and Dave also began telling their children who *they* were as kids. We think it's important for kids to know that their parents are people with troubles and problems just like theirs and that their questions, troubles, and problems are completely normal. This doesn't mean we confess every boneheaded thing we ever did or wanted to do in high school (*Yes, Mommy thought about flashing the varsity basketball team, too!*). But in admitting some of our own flaws and mistakes, we help our kids feel more connected to their parents.

Julie always worried that Phillip, who as a cop obviously had to be a hard-ass at work, was a little too Great Santini at home. (Once, when he was a kid, he was left to mind his little sister. She wasn't listening to him, plus he wanted to go out with his friends for a while—so Phillip handcuffed her to the radiator. Julie prefers to think of this as an endearing cop-in-training story rather than a madman-brother story.) One evening, shortly after getting back together, Phillip and Julie were sitting at the dining room table. They heard a loud crash behind them. It was their daughter Madelyn, who'd fallen down a flight of stairs. Before we could respond, she jumped up and screamed at her big sister, "It didn't work, Lauren!" then tromped back up the stairs with large pieces of cardboard paper Scotch-taped to her arms. Apparently, Lauren had decided it would be fun to have her six-year-old sister test the theory of whether a human could fly with a) cardboard wings affixed to her arms and b) enough momentum to get her started.

Julie started to shush Phillip, because she assumed he was going to start berating Lauren. But she stopped herself and instead said nothing. Even if he didn't handle the situation exactly as she would, she realized his way of dealing might be as valid as hers.

Phillip did not let her down. Instead of screaming and rushing to punish Lauren, he said calmly, "Don't ever do that again." And then to Lauren and Madelyn: "Did I ever tell you about the time I jumped off the garage with a trash bag for a parachute?"

Since we stopped coming in between our husbands and our children, we know one another better and deeper than we did before. Instead of translating, the children ask questions when they are confused or want more information and our husbands do the same. Now they hear it the way they need to and not the way we *think* they need to.

Even If You Think You Could Be Both Mother and Father to Your Child—Don't Try: Many of us are so invested in being independent, we take self-reliance just a little too far. We resent having to be Superwoman, but we play the part to the hilt. Because . . . well, you know what discourages many fathers from being more active participants in their kids' lives? The feeling that they're not needed.

Donna recalls vividly an argument with Dave about being a Scout leader for their son, Philip. The parents had been informed that if they did not become involved in the Scouts, the kids would not have a troop; there were simply not enough volunteers. When Donna came home from the meeting, she told Dave he had to sign up. After all, wasn't this a great male-bonding thing, an opportunity for him to convey all his camping skills to his son (as compared to Philip's mother, whose camping skills consisted of dialing the number of a four-star hotel)? Dave replied he didn't really know how to be a Scout leader, and wouldn't it be better if Donna did it?

Anyone who knows Donna knows two things: 1) She has a Wonder Woman complex; and 2) the prospect of camping with eight-year-old boys, learning to read the direction moss grows on a tree to lead them out of the wilderness if they were lost, was her idea of hell.

She wondered why Dave couldn't understand that life was about taking some risks, putting yourself out there, and learning new things. Throw yourself in and figure it out! No one tells us how to do many of the things we accomplish in life. What was he expecting . . . an instruction booklet?

Dave dug in his heels. He would not do it. Donna ended up being an assistant Scout leader for four years.

But Donna learned. After Dave left the house, Donna learned the usefulness of one of the oldest tricks of marriage—and, in fact, a trick her husband had been using on her: feigned helplessness.

Donna had no clue how to operate any photographic equipment more complicated than a point-and-shoot. Surely, she could have learned, just as she learned how to be a Scout leader. Instead, she told Dave that if their children were going to have any memories of their childhoods, it was up to him—Operator of All Things with Play, Stop, and Pause Buttons—to provide them. And guess what—it worked!

Practice Contingency Planning: Many of us have Hallmark-card notions about parenthood: We need to attend every game and school recital, and be our children's own personal cheerleading squad.

In truth, of course, we often fall short of the ideal. Work pressures mean we really can't stop and see the school play; maybe we can't afford the trip to Disney World this year. Donna and Julie often found themselves disappointed when their husbands fell short of their idealized versions of fatherhood. Friends would say, "Well, if he *really* wanted to be at her ballet recital, he would." And in fact, that's not true. Unless your husband is a real jerk, he's disappointed, too.

Over time, we realized there were options that still accomplish the same goal. Dad can't get to the big game? The game can be taped and watched together, at home, later that night. Maybe Disney World is out of reach but being together for a three-day road trip to see the World's Biggest Ball of Twine in Kansas or the largest bat colony in the world (in Texas, natch) is doable.

Our friends with the four-year-old twins just had a hellish summer, where work prevented them from going anywhere. But they learned, quite quickly, that it doesn't take a trip to the Galápagos to thrill two four-year-olds. And thus was born the Urban Safari: Every night, Dad would don his flak jacket and take the boys into the basement with a flashlight to find rats, mice, and cockroaches. Urban Safari became their favorite summer pastime. Oddly enough, their mom didn't participate.

Our point here is this: The goal is not being "correct," it is bringing Dad and kids together, in whatever form that takes.

Keep Dad in the Loop: For us, living in separate residences was an excellent communication catalyst, because we had to tell Dave and Phillip what was on the kids' calendars, and they had to keep track at their homes. But even for couples happily living together, keeping school and activity calendars in clear sight helps fathers feel involved. Julie, who feels about Excel the way Bogie felt about Bacall, has charts for every occasion. On the following page is a simplified activity chart (Julie's real chart . . . you don't want to know).

Category	Goal/Project	Frequency	Goal or 1st Time	Last Completed	Next Deadline	On Track	Next Steps
2005 Goals	Start/Catch Up Kids' College Savings and Retirement (Plan)	2005 Goal	August 2005	07/01/05	September 31, 2005	Yes	
	More Time at Home (Better Mom)	2005 Goal	Dec 2005	TBD	August 31, 2005	Yes	
	Pay off Family Debt (Cash Flow)	2005 Goal	Dec 2005	06/30/05	August 31, 2005	Yes	
Career	Update Resume and References	Biannual	N/A	01/21/05	September 1, 2005	Yes	
	Look at Marketplace to See What's Available	Quarterly	N/A	07/15/05	September 1, 2005	Yes	
	Organizations to Join	Annual	N/A	07/01/05	October 31, 2005	Yes	
Health: Family and Pets	OB/GYN	Annual	N/A	05/19/05	December 15, 2005	Yes	
	Dentist Appt	Annual	N/A	02/20/05	October 15, 2005	Yes	
	Optometrist/Contacts	Annual	N/A	09/15/04	September 1, 2005	Yes	
Financial	Credit Reports	Annual	N/A	04/04/05	April 15, 2006	Yes	
	College Savings Plans	Annual	N/A	07/01/05	September 31, 2005	Yes	
Travel/ Vacations/ Camps	Hilton Head Vacation	Annual	N/A	10/22/04	Fall 2006	Yes	
	Florida Vacation	Annual	N/A	07/09/05	Summer 2006	Yes	
Social/Hobby	Volunteers at Hospital	Maintain	N/A	N/A			
	Bingo Events	Maintain	N/A	N/A			
	Scrapbooking	Maintain	N/A	N/A			
Regular Occurring	Buy Birthday Cards/Mail Gifts	Quarterly	N/A	N/A	N/A	N/A	
	USPS	Weekly	N/A	N/A	N/A	N/A	
	Dry Cleaning	Weekly	N/A	N/A	N/A	N/A	
	Grocery Store Trip	Weekly	N/A	N/A	N/A	N/A	

Julie is also deeply enamored of her Reminder chart:

✳ REMINDERS AND HOUSE TO-DO LIST ✳

PHILLIP PROJECT
Put Wood Border around 4 windows (2 in Madelyn's, 2 in Master)
Frame Door in Master Bedroom
Replace Windows in Kitchen
Replace Window in Lauren's Room
Garbage Disposal
Fix Lamp I LOVE on the Porch
Finish Painting the Ceiling in Madelyn's Room and Put Up Trim

JULIE PROJECT
Buy pHaze Potion for my Face
Get Stickers for Inside Mady's Books
Get Birthday List Organized
Get Pictures Backed Up on CDs
Find Parachute Portrait for Living Room
Curtains for Dining Room / Kitchen
Finish Sorting and Labeling Kids' Clothes and Put Away
Sort/Clean Basement Closets

By placing charts like these in plain sight, family life becomes more accessible for everyone. Julie also created duplicate calendars for the workplace, to be updated regularly. (Send him e-mails if he works in an office environment, or simply use notes if he's got the calendar pinned up in his store, garage, hospital, etc.) We like notes. Notes in the calendar itself, brightly colored paper sheets cleverly placed in his wallet, in his briefcase, in his pants pocket, Post-its on the bedpost, in his car, on his forehead. Whatever works.

Forced awareness of the children's daily activities was half the battle. When they knew, there was no excuse for not taking part—and divvying up the activities, too. Donna, for example, might say Chelsea had a birthday party to go to, and Dave would stop and buy a present. And it would be an appropriate present, too—Dave would actually remember, for instance, the gender of the child having the birthday, thus insuring little Emily with her princess obsession got a Cinderella tea set rather than the Power Ranger he might have bought her in the past.

When it comes to managing the kids' schedules, Donna and Dave often take the "divide and conquer" approach to teamwork. On any given Saturday, there are undoubtedly several sporting events during the day for each of their children, and timing hardly ever works smoothly; there are usually overlaps, and they would have to clone each other in order to both attend each event. They try to have a family breakfast together and strategize as to who will be accompanying who where and make a plan to meet at an event or for lunch, before the events of the afternoon. In the fall, any given Saturday in the Browns' home goes like this:

- Power breakfast of Starbucks and bagels.
- Everyone goes to Chelsea's in-line hockey game.
- Philip (Donna and Dave's son) brings his gear, because halfway through Chelsea's game, Philip changes into his gear and goes with Dave to his game (Dave coaches both kids' teams, so this can be a little tricky—the park district organizer swore to us that she'd schedule the games at the same location to avoid this, but no dice).

- Donna stays with Chelsea at her game and then meets Dave and Philip at Philip's game at about halftime.
- After Philip's game is over, they meet at home for showers.

And that's all before lunch.

Depending when Philip's ice hockey game is, they might get everything done at home or they might be on the road, with lunch on the go. In spring, this schedule—which according to them is not too bad—is complicated further by floor hockey (there is no variety of hockey that is neglected in the Brown household) and Chelsea's baseball games. While it may seem frantic, this is the ultimate in teamwork!

Assume Areas of Responsibility. Then Stick with Them: Sometimes, feminism can trip us up. Take this notion that all household duties should be split fifty-fifty. Why? Why don't we just admit there are some things we're better at, and some things our husbands are better at—and sometimes (shudder) they're divided across stereotypical gender lines?

One of the blessings of our separation was that it allowed our husbands to figure out what tasks they were best at, and which ones were best left to us. Of course some duties of parenthood— picking up kids, attending plays and PTA meetings, selecting child care—were either dealt with by both of us or divided fifty-fifty. (Whoever was better at the particular homework assignment, for example, would monitor it. Julie covered reading and math, Phillip covered anything that involved, say, building a castle out of macaroni or the 500 other ridiculous crafty assignments children are forced to do on a weekly basis.) And Julie learned, through bitter experience, that entrusting Phillip to get the children's hair cut was tantamount to saying: "Kids, we'd like you to be mocked by your peers for the next month!" But while she has not relinquished control over their hair, she has learned to allow Phillip his taste in other areas of the kids' lives.

Both of our husbands, we discovered, were better at getting kids to comply with chores than we were—because if we were softies for our men, we were even more so for our wee ones. We often had favored-parent status, because we'd rather do something *for* our children than have them follow through. Or we'd make up consequences that didn't really exist so that we didn't have to be the bad guys. (Chelsea still half-believes that a monster will come and spirit away her dolls if she doesn't pick them up off the floor.) But anyone who has small children knows, it's the parent who lays down the law who gets the respect—and ultimately the love, too.

Prioritize: When our mates start becoming more engaged with the family again, many of us are so thrilled we forget that the husband is just one small human. We start lobbing tasks at him, because finally! We! Have! A! Partner! "Honey, can you mow the lawn? Honey, can you teach our daughter free throws? Honey, we need to buy a new entertainment center, can you come with me to . . . ?" It's sort of like having an ace staffer who's been on leave for six months: You're so grateful he's back you want him to do *everything*.

We arrived at our own decisions about priorities, and you'll have to come to yours. (This is where the four-block really comes in handy.) For us, anything having to do with the kids came first. If the choice was, mow the lawn or teach the free throws, the grass would have to look raggedy for a while. You might come to a different decision, but what's important is making the decision. Throw too much at him, and he's likely to retreat again.

We admit that we have not reached some stage of parenting nirvana, where we are in lockstep with each other about all parenting decisions. For example, Dave and Donna are both heavier than they'd like to be and still argue about nutrition for their kids; Donna has banned fast food from their lives, and Dave thinks Donna should lighten up. Julie, who grew up without much money and still winces at the memory of being the kid with the "wrong" jeans or sneakers, is much more lenient and spendy than Phillip on her teenage daughter's clothing.

But we have worked hard to balance these differences—and in a sense we're glad we *have* differences, because at least that means our husbands have strong opinions about fatherhood.

Phillip was an MIA parent who rarely showed up at events unless Julie begged, pleaded, and nagged. Today, he harasses HER to show up: She constantly hears, "You know it's important to them that you come, right?" and, "I hope you're going to be on time." Julie has no intention of missing anything, yet Phillip still calls and bugs her: "Are you leaving work yet? I think traffic is bad today." (Ironically, he has also upped the ante on Julie's chart obsession. He writes daily customized chore lists for the children.)

Phillip is also the one who went to 100 percent of Lauren's basketball games last year. Granted, there were only two games, but Julie's not one to quibble. He even videotaped them. Of course, they still have to work out a few rough spots. Whereas the "old Phillip" would have never gone, the "new Phillip" can now be heard on tape, mumbling to himself, "Why won't she raise her arms?" and "She's doing it all wrong." But he's got the right idea! Too bad Julie can never show Lauren the tape.

Today, Dave is brilliant. He is much more engaged and takes risks that he never would have before. He is a full participant in their family life. He coached Chelsea's baseball team and Philip's in-line hockey team. And with these teams, Donna purposefully stays uninformed about everything except game times so she can't swoop in to manage the process; Dave is fully capable of managing the teams himself without "suggestions" from her.

For Father's Day, Chelsea made a card for Dave thanking him for being her baseball coach and taking time out to do it with her. Donna recalls catching Dave's eye as he read his cards and the two of them sharing a knowing smile while their eyes welled up a bit. These are the moments you dream about when you think about your man as a father.

Recently, Julie was so proud when Madelyn honored Phillip by awarding him with the Hero of the Year Award detailing why he is such a great dad. A moment any dad would be proud of, but for Phillip it was finally proof that he had become the dad he wanted to be.

Our husbands became changed—and much happier—men when they regained focus on their children.

CHAPTER 5

Celebrate

Become a Believer in Ritual

· · · · ·

When humans participate in ceremony, they
enter a sacred space. Everything outside of that
space shrivels in importance. Time takes on a
different dimension. Emotions flow more freely.
The bodies of participants become filled with the
energy of life. . . . All is made new; everything
becomes sacred.

—SUN BEAR (NATIVE AMERICAN HEALER),
*Black Dawn, Bright Day: Indian Prophecies for
the Millennium That Reveal the Fate of the Earth*

Forget that time she did in the pokey: Martha Stewart is still an
influential figure in American culture. But why? Few people
really have a burning desire to, say, carve potatoes wedges into
flowers, then dip them in ink to create personalized gift stamps.
(This is an actual Martha project. Nothing we could make up
would be as, ah, unique as what she comes up with.) But Martha
speaks to our yearning for family tradition and rituals—and

gives us the tools to perform them. Even those of us with zero time like to think that once a year we can create a Thanksgiving feast worthy of Martha. Or that at some point in our lives we'll sit down with our children and create ribbon organizers. (They involve a shoebox, a dowel, and some grommets. Don't ask.)

Call us stupidly old-fashioned or just girly: We believe that celebrating holidays, anniversaries, and birthday parties are the mortar of home life. And our belief is supported by solid research. A 2002 review of studies published in the *Journal of Family Psychology* found that family routines—everything from eating together at dinnertime to going on vacations together to celebrating family holidays—correlate strongly with marital satisfaction, a sense of identity in adolescents, stronger family bonds, academic achievement, and even children's health. (One study found that children who had regular bedtime routines got to sleep sooner and woke up less frequently during the night than those with less regular routines. Household routines have even been found to shorten bouts of respiratory infections in infants.)

And of course we're not just talking about celebrating holidays. A ritual can be anything the kids/family look forward to that's done on a regular basis. It's something that may take a bit of time but costs nothing. A husband of one of our friends starts the day with his young boys the same way every morning: They get up, open the window, and count passing airplanes for twenty minutes before the day gets underway. Why do the boys love it so? Who knows? But they do, and it gets their day off to a great start.

OUR SCORECARD FOR CELEBRATING TRADITIONS

· Help plan birthday parties
· Help pick out and wrap birthday gifts
· Attend children's birthday parties and participate in games
· Help pick out Halloween costumes
· Participate in pumpkin carving
· Help pick out and address holiday cards
· Sign cards with your own name
· Help shop for holiday gifts
· Help wrap, pack, and mail presents as necessary
· Help build family gingerbread house
· Attend holiday events with family
· Help be Santa Claus
· Help decorate Christmas tree (or hide the afikomen)
· Help make valentines with kids
· Help decorate Easter eggs with kids
· Help make Easter baskets
· Help be the Easter bunny
· Help ensure the family eats together

⁎ **Celebrate Good Times, C'mon:** ⁎
Your Scorecard

STEP ONE—Prioritize: List all the ways you'd like your husband to participate more in the family rituals. Fill them in on their proper place on your four-block chart, identifying which items are of highest priority for you. Our Relationship Map for Family Rituals looked like this:

★ OUR RELATIONSHIP MAP: FAMILY RITUALS ★

LEVEL OF DISSATISFACTION

ND
- Help pick out and address holiday cards
- Sign cards with your own name
- Help shop for gifts
- Help decorate Easter eggs with kids
- Help make Easter baskets
- Help be the Easter bunny

ID
- Attend holiday events with family
- Help wrap, pack, and mail presents as necessary
- Help ensure the family eats together
- Help plan birthday parties
- Help pick out and wrap birthday gifts

NS
- Attend children's birthday parties and participate in games
- Help pick out Halloween costumes
- Participate in pumpkin carving

IS
- Help make valentines with kids
- Help build family gingerbread house
- Help be Santa Claus
- Help decorate Christmas tree (or hide the afikomen)

IMPORTANCE

STEP TWO—Filter: Take the items in the upper right quadrant of your four-block—the items of highest importance and greatest dissatisfaction.

For each item, ask:

- Is there a one-time fix to this issue? (Maybe he's just too lazy to go out and get the right pumpkin but would be happy to carve it if it arrives in the house. You get the pumpkin, he'll probably be happy to wield the cutting tool.)

- Can I fix this with technology or a new product that is on the market? (For instance, if one of your bugaboos is that your husband does not send cards to anyone, can you introduce him to the joys of online card companies such as Evite?)

These are the items you can handle. Set them aside. For all others in the upper right-hand quadrant, continue to step three.

STEP THREE—Analyze: For items that remain, you'll need to develop an approach to fixing them. Determine whether an item is going to be easy or hard to fix by asking yourself the following questions:

- Is my husband going to be cooperative on this issue? (There are some issues that might be solved by a well-planned conversation, but others where you know that your partner will be entrenched in his point of view, custom, or cultural perspective.)
- Do we (my husband or I) have the skills necessary to properly address this issue?
- Has this been an issue for less than one year?
- Can the task be done by only one person?

If you answered "yes" to all of these—we would call your problem easy. If you answered "no" to any of the questions—your problem would be considered hard.

For Easy Problems: We recommend approaching your husband with a recommendation and a quick conversation. If, for example, you and your husband come from different religious values, he may not be averse to celebrating your religious traditions, but may need some coaching to know what to do.

For Hard Problems: We recommend that if your husband isn't cooperative, prep work may be needed in order to gain agreement or compliance. If the problem is radically different backgrounds, you may need some counseling to become more comfortable with each other's traditions.

STEP FOUR—Plan Your Approach: In Donna's family, the idea of everyone sitting down to dinner together was a huge issue. Dinner was by necessity rushed, since the kids had various sports practices to go to afterward—and it seems there were always arguments about who ate what. She found herself ordering takeout from several different places to appease different appetites. Donna loathed that sense of fragmentation, where no one seemed to know what was going on—and no one seemed all that interested—in other family members.

Her solution? First, cutting down hugely on takeout. Since there wasn't much time for cooking, she discovered the joys of the crockpot—food cooks all day, and then there's just rice or noodles or potatoes to prepare at dinner. Second, no more catering to individual tastes. There would be one meal, and one meal only. If people had special requests, they got to "order" that request once during the week, and everyone else would have to abide. Third, splitting up tasks: a rotating chart where everyone had ONE chore (setting table, stacking and running dishwasher, emptying dishwasher, etc) a night. And finally, every night they would play one game that would elicit more than grunts from the family when Donna asked "What's new?" It might be, for example, what she called the "high/low game"— everyone had to say the high of their day, and the low of their day. Playing a game seemed stilted at first, but after a lot of eye-rolling it genuinely helped elicit conversation; one "silly" game would lead to a host of interesting topics. People in the family began looking forward to dinners.

CORE STRATEGIES FOR SUCCESS:
- **Project Management**
- **Recognition, Both Private and Public**
- **Culture Shaping (What is the "culture" you're trying to create at your home?)**

We grew up in families that never missed an opportunity for a celebration, particularly around the holidays. The decorations, the food, the family and friends—all of it defines who we are. When the rituals aren't in place, family life just feels sterile.

It doesn't matter what you choose to celebrate, or how; what matters is *having* rituals to begin with. And we're not just talking about special-occasion rituals: We're talking about creating all the little moments—eating meals together, reading to kids before bedtime, Saturday movie night—that define you as a family.

If you are a stay-at-home mother who has at least some time to devote to setting the domestic agenda, great; this is perhaps part of your job description. But more and more often, when two incomes are necessary, Mom is stressed-out, work becomes all-consuming, and family life becomes fragmented. Almost everyone going through a rocky time in their marriage has stopped creating rituals that define them as a family. We had to learn how to celebrate again, and we needed our husbands to be involved in the process.

In fact, one of the first signs our marriages were in trouble was when our husbands abdicated all responsibilities for family traditions. While Donna, a lapsed (but still guilty) Catholic, is not a believer in organized religion, Julie and Phillip are both religious—yet it was Julie who brought the kids to church each week. At Halloween, we mothers picked out the costumes (Julie even made them a few times); we made the Easter baskets, shopped for the presents, and planned every holiday.

Donna is not a card sender. She recalls a discussion with Dave early on in their marriage where Dave said that they should send out Christmas cards. Donna said, "Great! I'll give you my address book." In thirteen years of marriage, the pair never sent a card. But that was OK; it was one area of their life where there were no arguments.

However, to Julie, card sending is critical. She sends them for every holiday, including all the dumb fabricated ones used to plump up Hallmark's bottom line. (That one "Happy Earth Day!" card you received? That would be from Julie.) She believes people who are dear to her can't be praised or celebrated enough; if the stores were selling "Congratulations on your Menopause!" cards, she'd probably be buying those, too.

In the past, Phillip, not surprisingly, considered sending cards too much work. Yet without fail, when they were ready to walk into a family event where he hadn't seen someone in a while, he'd lean over and whisper to Julie, "We sent them a card, right?" "Yes, Phillip." "And did you send them a picture of the kids?" "Yes, Phillip." She would always sign *Julie and Phillip* in her own handwriting. It was a little irksome. Julie already had a boss at work; she didn't need to be her husband's personal secretary, too. One day she decided: *Enough.* I'm not signing for him. He'll have to send out his own cards.

To Julie, that was like taking off her wedding ring.

Donna, while spiritual, is not a churchgoer. However, for each of us, faith was mostly irrelevant when it came to celebration; it wasn't as if we needed our husbands to become any more or less religious than they already were. What we needed was a sense of having an experience that both connected us to our outside community and helped define us to one another as a family unit. The combination of the universal experience with a touch of the unique and personal: That's what rituals are about.

Still . . . where was it written that it was our job, and ours alone, to give our kids a sense of family? Why were *we* not only the designated party givers, but the social secretaries?

Well, here's one reason: We had such set-in-stone notions about how everything family-related was to be done, we gave our husbands little leeway for their own preferences. OK, no leeway. We'd written the scripts and directed the movie. And God forbid our vision was not *their* vision.

We also made family events more uncomfortable than they had to be by doing something so many women in troubled marriages do: Pretend everything is fine. Now, our families are gossips. But guess what? ALL families are gossips. And, as we learned, the best thing you can do to feed family gossip is to be uncomfortable and cagey at family functions.

We took the time to figure out what would bring the guys back into the fold with family occasions—what would make them want to help us?

Well, most important, it was allowing for the very real possibility that their version of the perfect family occasion might be notably different from ours. Sometimes they wanted events to be more low-key, sometimes more of a production.

Dave, for example, was a huge present giver and would always spend more than he could really afford. Still, the gift giving was very important to him, right up there in the upper right quadrant of the four-block scale. So again, we had to learn to step back and allow our husbands to direct the show sometimes. We each picked events that were most important to us. And then we allowed that there could only be one boss.

When Julie gave a party for her daughter Lauren, for instance, it tended to be, um, heavily themed. One year it was a "Royalty for a Day, Women That Rule" party. Each girl had to dress up as royalty, and when the guests arrived they were given a title and description of who they were (Queen Elizabeth, Indira Gandhi, Margaret Thatcher). Julie had her best friend fly in from Cincinnati and take pictures of the girls dressed up on a throne.

Phillip was AWOL.

Two years later, when he did the party, he took everyone to play laser tag.

In the past, Julie might have insisted he do the party her way. But—and we know you'll all be shocked to hear this—the girls loved playing laser tag way more than they loved playing Margaret Thatcher. Learning to let go also meant allowing for the very real possibility that the easy, convenient way was also sometimes the best way.

Though we did not express this explicitly to our husbands, we began to think of family occasions in terms of project management. Doing so accomplished two goals. One, we had a concrete strategy for the events themselves. And two, by setting the agenda ourselves—being the "big picture" organizers—we were more comfortable letting them put their own stamp on the particulars of any given occasion. It was as if we ordered the blank canvases and paint . . . then left them alone to paint their pictures. Sometimes we liked the pictures and sometimes we didn't, but we always managed to get them much more interested in the process, and the outcome, than if we had told them that the sailboat belonged over in the right side of the ocean, and the sun had to be *this* shade of gold, and the color of the water should be . . .

These were our general principles for bringing our husbands into the fold for family events of all sorts:

What's Your Family Culture?: In a corporation, so-called culture shaping is important, because every company's culture is unique. If you work at Disney, for example, you should be prepared to embrace the idea that you are all part of some grand yet wholesome theatrical experience for anyone who comes in contact with the company. (Former CEO of Disney Michael Eisner would start mass e-mails to employees with "Dear Cast Members." If you work at one of the parks, there are rules for everything from the length of your fingernails to the kinds of communication you can have with visitors. Which of course makes sense, particularly if you're in a Donald Duck costume.)

So it's critical to decide with your partner what kind of family culture you are trying to build together—and then consider how the rituals you're trying to establish contribute to, or take away from, that culture. If, for example, it's important to you that your children have a deep appreciation for the natural world, maybe you're better off taking the annual family vacation in Yellowstone National Park rather than New York City. Or if you want your kids to be lovers of art and artists themselves, you might decide that sending them to school in spotless clothes you're going to have to worry about isn't such a good idea, since art is, and should be, messy.

When Planning an Event, Figure Out the Participants and the Ultimate Goal: Is it the kids? You and your husband? Extended family? How will success be measured? (Great meal? Nobody gets drunk and drowns in the pool?) And how much time/money/angst can we allot to this particular occasion?

Inch by Inch It's a Cinch: The "project manager" can set the goal and give general ideas about how that goal should be accomplished. It is then up to the other spouse to realize that goal. But no arguing about the particulars. If, for example, you say, "Let's have a barbecue," you cannot tell him what to barbecue or what kind of marinade to use. Your husband needs to feel that this is a collaborative process; the barbecue becomes as much his event as yours.

Communicate, Communicate, Communicate: Don't make assumptions about what your husband wants—and tell him not to make assumptions about you.

Avoid the 3000-Degree Turkey: In business parlance, "the 3,000-degree turkey" concept goes like this: You can cook a turkey for ten hours at 300 degrees or for one hour at 3,000 degrees. Meaning that if you try to do all the work yourself, you end up with . . . a charred hulk of a turkey. When there's an event, one person may be the director, but every hand's on deck in a family. Particularly when you're talking about occasions just for the family . . . even the littlest person can fold napkins, or hit the POPCORN button on the microwave for Movie Night.

Turn Obstacles into Opportunities: How can you make a family event fun and creative within the time/budget constraints you have? For example, if money is tight in the summer, the annual July Fourth barbecue can always become "Bring Your Own Meat." (OK, beer. But we always kind of wanted a bring-your-own-meat party.)

Stand Tall with Your Family: With any celebration, you want it to be great for them *first*. And of course, while so many family traditions have become "all about the children," it's the husbands we're trying to get on our side. Lots of times family events become so chaotic we forget the person who's in the trenches with us. So take the time to have a private moment with your mate: a toast to each other in the kitchen, a private love-you message on the day of the event in his e-mail . . . or maybe some quick early morning thank-you sex. (We are not kidding. In our post-separation experience, we found out that the single best predictor of calm and cheerful cooperation on any big family day was . . . that first time together in the morning.)

The Team Is the Key to Success: Whether at work or home, there is something about knowing you've accomplished something, about feeling part of a team/family, that raises morale and self-worth. And this is true even when things go horribly wrong. Our friend Joan, who is to cooking what FEMA is to emergency response, put together an elaborate brunch for some out-of-town friends, and she enlisted the aid of her husband and family. It would take too long here to explain how collaborating on popovers resulted in enough smoke from a stove fire to clear out the entire floor of their apartment building, but suffice it to say it did, and her family and guests ended up shivering outside, while her kids and husband, tipsy from cheap mimosas, tried to explain what happened to the firemen. It was one of those events where, years later, if anything went wrong in some small annoying way, one member of the family only had to say, "Popovers" to make everyone laugh . . . because no matter how off-track something was going, chances are it wouldn't result in almost burning down half their apartment.

One of the first signs for Julie that Phillip was trying to get their marriage back on track was Phillip's change in attitude toward cards. During their separation, Phillip didn't just sign the cards, he and Julie actually MADE them together. (They were hideous. But the couple began signing together again.)

Sometimes we're perversely fonder of our failures than our successes. Teamwork, successful or not, can help define you as a family unit.

Learn as You Go and Act on What You Know: With any luck, every "project" (i.e., the Easter egg roll, the Seder, etc.) that was completed taught us a lesson. Of course, sometimes the lesson was, "Oh my God, what was I thinking with that garlic shrimp?" or "Never invite Aunt Sadie again." But whatever it was, it invariably brought us together as a family.

There Is No Such Thing as Too Much Praise: It's a bit of a cliché, but it's true: You can pretty much get men to do the same thing over and over if you make a big ol' fuss about it. But when is the last time you lavished praise on your husband without a note of criticism, too? Julie realized, for example, that this year if Phillip takes the kids to get Halloween costumes, she should thank him instead of asking why on earth he got the stupid Dracula costume for Hunter when she thought he should be Yoda. WRONG APPROACH. Essentially, Julie was guaranteeing that, next year, Phillip wouldn't want to help.

Instead, the key to roping him into the family behavior you want is praise for every little step of the process. "Thanks for thinking about what the kids should wear." "Thanks for taking them to get the costumes." "Thanks for making them try on the costumes." And secondarily, make your praise public: Let your husband overhear you praising him to others. Julie believes that her son Hunter would make an adorable Dracula, even if it's not her first choice, and Julie will be quick to tell everyone within earshot that it was All Phillip's Idea.

True, if she were doing this with a work colleague it would be sucking up. But we all do it to some degree with work colleagues, and we all see that it actually yields results.

The special events—all that card sending, all those bunnies and Santas and pumpkins—were all very well, but the single most important ritual we insisted our husbands reinstate when we got back together was . . . dinner. Having dinner as a family had gone by the wayside as our marriage deteriorated. More often than not, each family member was eating dinner while watching TV . . . sometimes alone in their own rooms. Often the kids were away with their friends.

It felt awful—and plenty of research on family life indicates that not eating together really IS awful for the family. According to the National Center on Addiction and Substance Abuse, children who never eat dinner with their families are over *60 percent more likely to smoke, drink, or use illegal drugs.* On the flip side, teens who eat with their families at least five times a week are less likely to do drugs or be depressed and are more likely to be motivated in school, according to a study presented at the American Psychological Association. Families who eat together also are more than twice as likely to eat the recommended number of five fruits and vegetables daily. And perhaps most important, eating together is where much of the talking takes place and where we can get to know one another better.

Or, in our cases, where we got to re-know each other. During our separation, as our husbands completed more and more of the Scorecard, they got to spend more time with us. Once-a-month dinners became once a week, then once every couple of days. They learned what we knew already: Even if little Chelsea had spilled the milk or Madelyn was eating with her mouth open, there's no substitute for breaking bread with the ones you love.

CHAPTER 6

Play

Become My Lover

• • • • •

There came a time when the risk to remain tight
in the bud was more painful than the risk it took
to blossom.

—ANAÏS NIN

We're betting that even those of you who purchased this book
not because your marriage is on the skids but simply because
there are a few areas you'd like to fix . . . well, we're betting you
turned to this chapter. Not only because sex is more innately
interesting than, say, lawn mowing, but because there is hardly
a married person alive who wouldn't like *something* about their
sex life to be better. We are all looking for sex advice that works
and also does not involve the words "Find someone new to have
sex with!" Because while that may be an option to make sex
more exciting, it's kind of a non-starter if you're interested in
things like integrity and marital satisfaction.

OUR SCORECARD FOR A BETTER SEX LIFE

···

- Get marriage counseling
- Take me on dates once in a while
- Dress to impress (me) occasionally
- Don't turn every back rub into sex
- Don't criticize me all the time
- Remember that I have feelings, too
- Pay attention to what I like
- Pay attention to what I say
- Pay attention to what I do
- Pay attention to what I need
- Respect what I don't like and don't want
- Don't make unilateral decisions. Remember that we have a partnership.
- Show interest in my work and my life as an individual
- Don't take out your anger about other problems on me

···

✳ I Can't Get No Satisfaction ✳ (Can I?): Scorecard

STEP ONE—Prioritize: List everything you feel would make your sex life richer and more satisfying. (Try to stay with things that are in the realm of possibility. Items like: "Have sex with George Clooney"? Probably not so possible. Fill them in on their proper place on your four-block chart, identifying which items are of highest priority for you.

★ OUR RELATIONSHIP MAP: LOVIN' ★	
ND • Remember that we have a partnership. • Show interest in my work and my life as an individual	**ID** • Get marriage counseling • Take me on dates once in a while • Don't turn every back rub into sex • Don't take out your anger about other problems on me • Don't criticize me all the time • Remember that I have feelings, too • Pay attention to what I like • Pay attention to what I say • Pay attention to what I do • Pay attention to what I need
NS • Occasionally dress like you're going to a job interview (and I'm the one in charge of hiring)	**IS** • Don't make unilateral decisions. • Repect what I don't like and don't want

LEVEL OF DISSATISFACTION *(vertical axis label)*

IMPORTANCE

STEP TWO—Filter: Take the items in the upper right quadrant of your four-block—the items of highest importance and greatest dissatisfaction.

For each item, ask:

- Is there a one-time fix to this issue? (That is, if your libido or his libido is low, there may be a *medical* issue that can be treated.)
- Can I fix this with technology or a new product that is on the market? (And for sexual dissatisfaction issues, there is no end to the new products available!)

These are the items you can handle. Set them aside. For all others in the upper right-hand quadrant, continue to step three.

STEP THREE—Analyze: For items that remain, you'll need to develop an approach to fixing them. Determine whether an item is going to be easy or hard to fix by asking yourself the following questions:

- Is my husband going to be cooperative on this issue? (There are some issues that might be solved by a well-planned conversation, but others where you know that your partner will be entrenched in his point of view, custom, or cultural perspective.)
- Do we (my husband or I) have the skills necessary to properly address this issue?
- Has this been an issue for less than one year?
- Can the task be done by only one person—and, in the case of sex issues, am I actually *happy* to take care of this myself?

If you answered "yes" to all of these—we would call your problem easy. If you answered "no" to any of the questions—your problem would be considered hard.

For Easy Problems: We recommend approaching your husband with a recommendation and a quick conversation. He may be dying to work something new into your sex life—and all it takes is a word from you to let him know you're as eager as he is.

For Hard Problems: We recommend that if your husband isn't cooperative, prep work may be needed in order to gain agreement or compliance. If neither of you has the skill set, you may need to go to training or pay someone else to do it (sex therapy, psychological counseling, etc.).

STEP FOUR—Plan Your Approach: Julie and Phillip had stopped spending any time together without the children. Mostly it came down to planning: There wasn't any. Eventually Julie realized that if they had to scramble for a babysitter at the last minute, they would end up staying home rather than going through the hassle of finding someone. So she began to think of their "together" time the way many of us think about manicures or hair highlighting . . . you just make a standing appointment for the same time every week (or month or whatever), and never have to worry about that appointment again. So Julie and Phillip booked a babysitter one night a week, for six months ahead of time. Occasionally they would use that time for something not so very romantic, like shopping. Sometimes they wouldn't leave the house; they'd tell their children they were going out, then go out the door, sneak back in, and hide in the bedroom. But more often they had a lovely dinner and saw a movie; they talked to each other, reconnected. Having a "standing" date night made all the difference.

> **CORE STRATEGIES FOR SUCCESS:**
> **Confidence Building (Yours and His)**
> **Positive Reinforcement**
> **Being Open to Change**

Did our marriages fall apart because our sex lives were lacking, or were our sex lives lacking because our marriages were falling apart? On this issue, husbands and wives tend to disagree. Ask our husbands, and they would say bad (or no) sex = the breakdown of a marriage. Ask us, and we'd reply that we didn't feel like having sex with someone who put about as much effort into his life as Homer Simpson.

Our husbands would retort that we didn't have as strong a sex drive as they do. Are they correct? Not exactly.

When it comes to sexual behavior, men and women are not as different as we once thought. A 2003 Ohio State University study demonstrated that the reason there seemed to be this huge gap in sexual interest and activity was simply that women were not 'fessing up to what they really thought and did. The study asked men and women about their behavior under various conditions—including when the participants thought they were hooked up to a lie detector. (Oddly enough, when they thought they could be caught lying, many women suddenly had more sexual partners and more sexual experimentation than previously reported. Men's answers didn't change that much whatever the circumstances.) The conclusion? "Women are sensitive to social expectations for their sexual behavior and may be less than totally honest when asked about their behavior in some survey conditions," said psychologist Terri Fisher, co-author of the study.

But then again . . . even if our behavior ultimately isn't so different from that of our male counterparts, it's more complicated for us to get to the point of actually wanting sex in the first place. Let's face it: Men can find everything about you intensely irritating yet still want to have sex with you. Women find irritation a libido-killer. And if we're not satisfied sexually, we're annoyed about *that*. At a certain point the annoyances of domestic squabbles and sexual dissatisfaction blend into one another, and the thinking becomes: *Hm, he can never find the milk in the refrigerator, so why should I be surprised he can't find my G-spot?*

Julie and Phillip always had a great sex life—once it started. But as she took on more and more of the responsibilities of family life, Julie was frequently exhausted—and this became her foreplay:

Phillip: Hey, do you want to . . .
Julie: No.

For Julie, anger was not exactly an aphrodisiac. And Julie was angry—a lot. There was very little in the way of a lead-up to sex . . . no kissing, no touching beforehand. Before she and Phillip got married, her panties matched her bras, her legs would always be shaved, and she would never be naked with socks. But as her marriage deteriorated, did she feel like making an effort? Let's just say that low-boiling fury that was always in danger of erupting did not make Julie feel like donning the French maid's uniform and prancing around the room.

Like Phillip, Dave began to feel that most of his marital problems revolved around Donna's lack of interest. If only she wanted sex, everything would be fine! And Donna's attitude was: If only he contributed to our marriage, our sex life would be fine!

Donna and Dave had the same problem as Woody Allen and Diane Keaton's characters in the movie *Annie Hall.* Both Annie and Alvy (Woody Allen's character) are talking with their therapists, and the question of how often they have sex comes up.

"Hardly ever," Alvy complains. "Maybe three times a week."
"Constantly," Annie sighs. "Probably three times a week." Donna
would take foreplay over the act of intercourse on most days;
she could have three orgasms just receiving a back rub. Needless to say, this didn't suit Dave, who judged the quality of his
marriage on the robustness of his sex life—his *intercourse sex*
life. Dave's motto during the bad years of their marriage might
as well have been, "It's the sex life, stupid." There was a huge
expectation gap: She wanted sex once or twice a week, and he
wanted it once or twice a day. In his mind, if they were in love,
they'd be doing it all the time. In her mind, love had nothing to
do with it. But if he had a) a job, b) a waistline (he'd gained fifty
pounds), and c) (most important) reengagement with his
family, there would be more nookie.

In fact, before he moved out, Dave started exercising and
lost fifty pounds thinking he would recapture what they had at
the beginning of their relationship. It was a valiant effort, and
he looked great; Donna thought they were having more, and
more experimental, sex. But his transformation never pro-
duced the results Dave desired, though he never told Donna
what those expectations were. After putting out all the effort into getting their marriage back on track and finding the
results did not match his expectations, he began to spiral into
depression.

But to Donna, being married to a hottie was not the point.
It would have been much better if the weight Dave lost was his
.5-ounce credit card as his spending was what was *really* weigh-
ing him (and Donna) down. Anger had gotten in the way of
lust—anger, and lack of respect.

By the time we kicked our husbands out, we were so shut
down to sex that we were both entertaining our Power Grrrrl

Commune Fantasy. This is where, post-divorce, we would move into a commune in Sedona, Arizona, with our close girlfriends and their children. We would share all the cooking and babysitting duties, while adding merrily to our investment portfolios with all the money we'd be saving. We'd eat anything we wanted, and men we met on dating services, selected entirely for their looks and mechanical ability, would come over once a week to have sex and fix things. Then they would leave.

As you can see, when it comes to sex it is rarely one person in the couple who has a problem; the problem lies with both partners. Thus the takeaway from this chapter is not, "Well, I fixed him!" When it comes to repairing one's sex life, *everyone in that bed needs to be fixed.*

Hey, we're not sex therapists. We're not going to give you a bunch of tips like, "Pretend your husband is a mysterious stranger and meet at a bar." You know what? People who are that good at acting *generally are actors.* We are not among those people. We look at our husbands trying to look brooding and mysterious in a bar, and in about thirty seconds we are laughing hysterically. So we'll leave that kind of advice to the seven trillion sex manuals on the market.

Still, we did manage to successfully get our sex lives back on track. How did we do it? Here are a few suggestions:

The Three E's: Explore, Experiment, Excite: Whether the bad patch in your marriage involves something as severe as actually separating or as minor as simply not feeling like touching your mate for a couple of weeks, we don't believe in celibacy. We are very much proponents of the use-it-or-lose-it school of sexuality. This isn't a license to go out and screw the first guy whose ad you read on Craigslist; in fact, this isn't a suggestion that you seek "extracurricular activities" at all. But there is an opportunity here to get in touch with your own sexuality, *apart from* that of your mate. When's the last time you went to a truly erotic movie? Cruised some Internet porn sites? (Our current favorite for erotic stories aimed at women: www.oystersandchocolate.com.) Bought a new sex toy? (There are dozens of new toys, by the way, that can hide in plain sight. Seen the Rubba Duckie? It's looks exactly like Ernie's favorite bathtub companion; it floats and it vibrates. Kind of cool, if you can get past the fact that you're being pleasured by a duck.) You've probably been so occupied with domestic minutiae, you've forgotten what turns you on.

Our point is simply this: You don't have to cheat to figure out some new things about yourself sexually.

Make Him Put Aside Fifteen Minutes a Day to Talk to You: We thought about calling this whole chapter, "Want Sex? Ask Me About My Day." Because, in a sense, asking about our day *is* foreplay. This is what we finally made our men understand. There were times where it didn't really matter if our husbands were genuinely concerned about what was going on in our lives; we would have been happy if they'd faked it.

In fact, we realized in retrospect that during the bad days of our marriages, our sex lives had fallen apart not from a failure of our bodies to connect but the failure of our brains. When Donna found out Dave was meeting a woman in a bar to pour out his heart because he felt he could talk to her, she was more upset than if they'd been having sex. Donna felt their big issue was that he wouldn't talk to her—and here he was, talking to someone else! It was, in her mind, a terrible betrayal.

And Julie remembers all too well how bad their communication had gotten. Phillip would say to her, "You never say you like how I look," "You never say you like my body"—things she honestly didn't think he cared about. In her mind, eroticism was a little about sexual contact, sure, but it was a lot more about romantic contact. Phillip could tell you to the day and to the hour the last time they had sex. For Julie . . . well, they might not have had sex for a month, but if Phillip stroked her hair when he walked by she'd be thinking, "God, I love him!" Because that's what makes her feel connected. And that's what Julie never got from her husband.

But the lack of communication was not entirely one-sided. Donna, for example, is trained professionally not to open up about her personal life, because in human resources she has the kind of job that requires knowing a great deal of personal information about staff, and the need to be private, and perhaps a little distant, has become second nature to her. She can't become too chummy with people, because the person she's lunching with today could be the same one she has to fire next week. It's dicey.

That tendency to keep everything close to the vest spilled over into Donna's sex life, too. She was simply not used to communicating her wants and needs, and she had to work very hard to open up.

When Dave and Phillip were finally made to understand that sitting down and talking was as important to us as actual sex was to them, it was a turning point for all of us.

"Not That There's Anything Wrong with That": Turn Off Your Internal Judge-and-Jury: True, not everyone can do this. Many of us have religious, ethical, or simply emotional reasons for being unable

to listen to our husbands discuss what is most exciting to them—
and our husbands may not want to hear what is most exciting
to us.

But sometimes it's possible to sit down and talk about your
fantasies with each other if you lay down the ground rules first.
And the important ground rule, for most of us, is simply this: It
is *fantasy*. Talking about being in bed with two women or men
at the same time; talking about being spanked or tied up or
eaten by bears or whatever the particular scenario is that turns
you on, *does not mean you're obliged to do it*. Many women are
frightened to talk to their men about fantasies because they believe that talking is the gateway to acting on it. For some of us it
is; for the vast majority, the fantasy is enough.

Be Open to Change: What if, at this point in your life, sex isn't that
high on your priority list? Well, barring medical impediments—
you've just had your gallbladder removed, you just had a baby—
you may have to change (a little). Remember this: As important
as it may be to you to make sure the socks next to the bed get
placed in the laundry hamper, *that's* how important it is to him
that they were flung there in a crazed ripping-off-your-socks
event. You can't ignore the fact that this may be an area of importance for your spouse. None of us was named Queen of
Priorities.

Julie and Phillip acknowledge that, even today, there's a certain quid pro quo to sex (though now they can laugh about it).
When Julie wants Phillip to do something with her he's not 100
percent comfortable with—going to a party with her, taking the
kids to the park by himself, hosting scrapbook night, whatever
thing she's concocted—she can get compliance by the promise
of sex. (And it IS a promise. And she follows through.) Phillip

likes to call his wife at work (when he knows she can't talk), tell her about some fabulous thing he's done for her, and describe, in extremely graphic detail, what she'll be doing for him later. (Julie calls it the lovin'-for-laundry program.)

Make It a Point to Compliment One Thing About Each Other's Appearance Every Day: This may seem kind of awkward at first—but not for long. Listen, you married this creature; even if it's not the best time in your life with him, even if he looks appreciably different than when you got married . . . there must still be things about him that appeal to you. We don't care if you're complimenting the length of his eyelashes or the smoothness of his elbows . . . just let him know you are still drawn to him.

Because, believe it or not, it's not only you who requires the compliments.

Then watch what happens. When you start noticing him positively, the compliments will flow more easily from him. Instead of a vicious cycle of criticism, you can launch a "kind cycle" of praise. Since Julie started pointing out to Phillip what she loved about his body, he's been much more forthcoming. The other day he commented on her shapely, full lips—how they were one of the things that originally attracted him to her. Despite being slightly irritated that he wasn't immediately compelled to marry her when he discovered her great PERSON-ALITY, she was moved to tears that he would take her on this mini-walk down memory lane.

(P.S: It also doesn't hurt to remember, occasionally, about the way you dressed and preened for your husband when you first got together. How many of the last five Valentine's Days did you shave your legs for your husband? You probably shaved them more carefully for your visits to the gynecologist.)

We're not suggesting you flounce around the house in an evening gown. But—well, what are you wearing right now? Would you ever, *ever* have let your husband see you like this when you started dating? No one except people in drawing room comedies of the 1940s can dress daily as if they're out on a first date. But you don't have to spend every day in a fuzzy orange sweat suit, either.

Did You Like It When He Did That Thing Last Night? Let Him Know: In this arena of marriage more than any other, enthusiasm counts. Did he do something you loved? Make noise. A lot of it. Did he do something you didn't like? You don't have to complain; you just have to not respond positively. "It really is like training a dog," one girlfriend said to Julie. "Occasionally, I've thought about buying one of those clickers and using it every time he hits my G-spot."

It's not just what you say, though, it's how you say it. And we're afraid that many men are trying cluelessly to compliment and they don't know how. It is your job to show them. As Julie explains:

> *Once Phillip gets me out of my everyday routine, I'm almost always into having sex. It's just that, like lots of women with sixty-hour work weeks and young kids, I have a lot of distractions, so sex is almost never at the forefront of my mind. So Phillip has had to become better at getting my attention, and I've become better at being more spontaneous. I think I've gotten to the point that I love surprising him . . . I suggest meeting in the bathroom or sneaking downstairs when everyone is upstairs, etc. And we have both become MUCH BETTER at letting each other know how to talk to the other. He's finally be-*

ginning to understand what I think of as "positive feedback," and what makes me uncomfortable.

Enthusiasm is a huge confidence builder—for both of you.

Apart from Sex Itself, Tell Him Exactly What You Need to Get Turned On: Yes. We know. "If he was really tuned into me he'd already know what I want." An excellent notion, except for the fact that IT'S WRONG. He can love you very much and not have a clue. It took Julie a very long time to accept the fact that mind reading and love were not the same thing. Lately, she simply started telling Phillip exactly what he needs to do outside the bedroom to make their sex life better. And often it doesn't revolve around sex. Recently, she told him, "Do you realize every single time you bring me flowers, you get sex? I must really like flowers." (Of course back rubs, Donna and Julie agree, are the epitome of progress. They do ask. And ask. Julie is pretty resigned to the fact that Phillip is incapable of being within six inches of her breasts without thinking he might get something out of it. Donna, on the other hand, says Dave has become a master masseuse and makes her quiver on a regular basis.)

The Answer to "Was It Good for You?" Is Sometimes, It Doesn't Matter: This is going to get us in trouble. Still . . . not every sexual encounter has to be a grand, romantic, passion-filled moment that takes three hours and ends with a screaming climax. Yes, that is nice. OK, it is really, *really* nice. But sometimes, you—or more to the point, he—just want to get off. If you wait endlessly for all the planets to align so that sex will be just right, you're not going to get a lot of action. And neither will he.

Don't get us wrong. Sometimes the guy is just as guilty of

putting up obstacles to sex. One of our friends, Amanda, explains it like this: "My husband complains we rarely have sex. The fact is, I've got three little kids, I work, and I'm tired a lot. But I'm *happy* to have sex much more often than we do if he just understands that I'm not always going to have an orgasm. He says it's not fun if I'm not 'into it' also. Like a lot of guys, he doesn't understand that a woman can enjoy sex sometimes—the touching, the closeness, everything about it—without climaxing. So in essence he makes me feel like I have to fake it for his ego—and *that* bugs me."

Julie has worked hard to get over her idea that "the moment has to be perfect"—and has started being more aggressive sexually, as Phillip has requested. Conversely, Phillip has worked hard to not turn every touch into an invitation for sex: He will sit next to Julie, stroke her hair, and that's enough. They both, each in their own ways, are taking the pressure off the other.

Forget Date Night—Try Date AFTERNOON: For lots of women, the whole "date night" thing is a bit of a joke. There's so much going on during the day that on date night all they want to do is crawl into bed and sleep—particularly after they've been out and had a good meal and a few glasses of wine.

So why not try a little afternoon tryst instead? For some reason, many women report being at their randiest at three or four PM And guess what, that's a time when it's easier to send the kids over to their grandparents' anyway. Also, do not underestimate the erotic value for your husband of being able to see you. You may feel best cloaked in the darkness of night, with that little pooch in your stomach safely shielded from sight. But remember that old saying: "A man falls in love through his eyes;

a woman, through her ears." He is hardwired to be turned on by visual stimuli (as every woman knows who has seen her husband hit the Close button on his computer screen when she walks into the room). So while you may be thinking, Ack, he'll see my cellulite, he's thinking, Yum.

Make Your Bed a No-Child Zone: We canvased our girlfriends who were in relatively happy marriages about the one thing that was preventing them from having more and better sex with their husbands. The immediate answer for those with young children was almost always "exhaustion," but a little further probing for those whose children were young but not outright babies was ". . . and of course the kids are always right there." Right where? "In bed with us."

It is one of the unspoken little secrets of American parenthood that tots are often in bed with their parents. "I always laughed at my big ol' hippie friends who advocated 'attachment parenting,' and 'the family bed,' where the kids are supposed to hang with the parents 24/7—even sleep with them," our friend Joan told us one day. "I always thought that was a joke. Then I had a son, and from the moment he could crawl out of his crib he was in bed with me and my husband. He's so sweet, the way he creeps in at night. I *still* think the whole 'family bed' thing is stupid, and yet here I am, in the damn 'family bed.'"

Children already put enough of a damper on your sex life by tiring you out during the day. Don't let them put the kibosh on the whole thing by actually being with you at night.

The Don't Ask/Don't Tell Policy: Let's say you do end up separating and later getting back together. Please pay attention to us on this one: As a subject of conversation, your dating life during the separation is off-limits. Sometimes for years, and possibly forever.

During our separations, we don't know what our husbands did, and we don't want to know. Well, that's not quite true. Donna knew enough about Dave's almost-affair to know that if there was more to it than he was admitting, it was too painful for her to know.

It's lovely to think the two of you could laugh over your experiences when you're back together, maybe even learn something. Lovely—and lethal. Sure, maybe you're the one-in-a-million person who won't be wondering, Did she have less cellulite than me? And maybe he won't be kept up nights thinking, The other guy's was bigger . . . it was bigger . . . I just know it. But you know what? Do you *really* want the pain that undoubtedly comes if you're not that one-in-a-million person?

So while a part of us wanted to know everything our mates were doing when we weren't around, well, we knew it was an area best left unexplored. We took to heart the Mafia code of *omerta* (the code of honor that prohibits indulging information about certain activities).

And if you do say anything—anything at all—lie. ("Yours is much bigger": Words to live by.)

No Casual Dates Meet Your Children. Ever: (Here, of course, we're talking to couples who are separated and divorced and have children.) Do we have to spell this out? Apparently we do, because we are always amazed at the number of people who bring their "new friends" to meet the kids after one or two dates. The excuse is generally, "Well, how can I ever be intimate with this person unless he stays with me?"

We don't care what you have to do. Go to his place, hire a babysitter and find a cheap motel . . . have a little afternoon delight while the kids are at school . . . do it in your *car*, for God's sake. But don't introduce new people—and by extension new issues to contend with—into the lives of kids who are already feeling at sea.

Now there's always the chance you'll keep your husband as your "friend with benefits" during a separation. This is, of course, a very individual decision. Some women report that during their separation, the sex was some of the best of their lives—even given the anger and unhappiness they experienced, the uncertainty of their futures added a certain frisson to the sex.

But while—as Donna put it—"I was very interested in having sex with someone other than myself," we did not sleep with our husbands while we were separated. They were already motivated to keep a toe in the door—and this would have been way more than a toe. So it seemed the kinder thing, for us *and* them, to stay out of the bedroom while we lived apart.

In this crucial arena for happiness, we've *all* had to learn more flexibility, more honesty—and playfulness. (Dave may not have the twice-a-day nookie he craves, but at least he gets more morning quickies in the shower. And Julie and Phillip get bonus points for Oscar-worthy role-playing: Julie bought and wore the skimpy Santa suit Phillip loved that came with accessories she eventually figured out were kneepads. And Phillip graciously indulged one of Julie's fantasies—and started coming to bed in his cop uniform.)

Objectively speaking, our husbands were attractive men even during the worst periods of our marriage. But we couldn't see it. We couldn't see anything appealing about a guy with a bad attitude who didn't contribute. Now, we look at them and think they're the sexiest things on earth, almost anytime: dirty, clean, fat, skinny, in sweats with holes in them . . . because it's not about the looks. It is, to a great degree, about their own self-confidence and about the respect we've regained for them.

CHAPTER 7

Share

Become a Domestic God

• • • • •

In a 1997 nationwide survey on changing gender roles conducted by Harvard University and the Henry J. Kaiser Family Foundation, most men surveyed said they were happy to share child care and domestic chores with wives who work outside the home. Happy? Nay, delighted!

Who are those men? Where do they live? Certainly not on this planet. The survey went on to say that despite the delight men take in ironing and picking Cheerios out of the shag rug, working mothers still do twice as much housework as their husbands, and more than half of all women questioned expressed at least some dissatisfaction with the amount of help their husbands provide around the house. Oh, and here's a jolly addendum to that survey: The suicide rate of professional women now is equal to that of men. See? At least we've got parity somewhere!

During some of the worst days of her marriage, Julie remembers the frustration of hearing so many people tell her what a great guy Phillip was. Great for picking up the kids when other dads didn't, great for being seen at the after-school daycare paying the weeky bills. But somehow, *she* managed to hold down a sixty-hour-a-week job and still pay attention to the home. When Phillip worked, the lawn was brown, the recycling piled up, and the children were in before-care and after-care programs.

For most of us, having a husband who's an equal partner in household chores is still something of a fantasy—but at least doing the Scorecard can move you in the right direction. We've said it before, and we'll say it again: It's not so much the sharing of tasks but the division of labor that should be your goal.

OUR DOMESTIC SCORECARD

- **Help with grocery shopping**
- **Help shop for household supplies**
- **Help with meal planning**
- **Share the cooking**
- **Share the dish washing**
- **Help do the laundry**
- **Pick up and drop off dry cleaning**
- **Help maintain family car (fill with gas, get oil changed, get car cleaned)**
- **Share the housecleaning chores**
- **Share the yard work**
- **Participate in house decorating decisions**
- **Help to buy furniture**
- **Take pets for vet visits**

✴ Peel Me a Grape . . . and Swiffer the Curtains: ✴
Your Scorecard

STEP ONE—Prioritize: List all the domestic chores you'd like him to do, either partially or totally. Fill them in on their proper places on your four-block chart, identifying which items are of highest priority for you.

✴ OUR RELATIONSHIP MAP: DOMESTIC GOD-HOOD ✴

LEVEL OF DISSATISFACTION

ND
- Pick up and drop off dry cleaning
- Participate in house decorating decisions
- Help to buy furniture
- Take pets for vet visits

ID
- Share the cooking
- Share the dish washing
- Help do the laundry
- Share the yard work
- Share the housecleaning chores

NS
- Help with meal planning

IS
- Help with grocery shopping
- Help shop for household supplies
- Help maintain family car (fill with gas, get oil changed, get car cleaned)

IMPORTANCE

STEP TWO—Filter: Take the items in the upper right quadrant of your four-block—the items of highest importance and greatest dissatisfaction.

For each item, ask:

- Is there a one-time fix to this issue (say, a housekeeper to come once or twice a month for the really big cleanups)?

- Can I fix this with technology or a new product that is on the market? (Endlessly irked by the husband who never puts a new roll of toilet paper on the dispenser? Invest in a dispenser that loads four to five rolls at a time.)

These are the items you can handle. Set them aside. For all others in the upper right-hand quadrant, continue to step three.

STEP THREE—Analyze: For items that remain, you'll need to develop an approach to fixing them. Determine whether an item is going to be easy or hard to fix by asking yourself the following questions:

- Is my husband going to be cooperative on this issue? (There are some issues that might be solved by a well-planned conversation, but others where you know that your partner will be entrenched in his point of view, custom, or cultural perspective.)
- Do we (my husband or I) have the skills necessary to properly address this issue?
- Has this been an issue for less than one year?
- Can the task be done by only one person?

If you answered "yes" to all of these—we would call your problem easy. If you answered "no" to any of the questions—your problem would be considered hard.

For Easy Problems: We recommend approaching your husband with a recommendation and a quick conversation. It's possible that he would be willing to do the laundry or load the dishwasher if you showed him how.

For Hard Problems: We recommend that if your husband isn't cooperative—prep work may be needed in order to gain agreement or compliance. If neither of you has the skill set, you may need to go to training or pay someone else to do it (frequent housecleaning service, for example).

STEP FOUR—Plan Your Approach: Making your husband into a domestic god is not only about getting him to do tasks he doesn't do; it's also learning about, and appreciating, the tasks he DOES do. We found that we were so focused on the negative, we simply didn't see the things that *were* getting done around the house, almost invisibly. So we tell everyone who thinks their husband is a layabout—and who disagrees with you, as they often do—to ask him if the two of you can switch household chores for just one day. You will both gain a different perspective—and often appreciation—for the other's role. Recently, when Phillip had a minor medical procedure, Julie had to tackle one job Phillip always reliably did: emptying the trash. She hadn't done this for ten years or more, and she was at a complete loss. Do the blue bags (recycling) go in the same bin with the black bags? Did they have trash bins? Where were they? She couldn't see them outside the window, and it was cold outside. The bag was too heavy; she couldn't get it out of the commercial-size trash-can she had in her kitchen. Why was it overflowing? Who threw the wrapper and missed the can? What the hell? *This job sucks.* Does this door lock from the inside or the outside? It takes THREE trips to take out the trash?

Julie became more and more frustrated, and finally, Phillip, who couldn't stand it anymore, jumped out of the bed (which he wasn't supposed to leave) and limped to the Dumpster with Julie. (Julie claims she protested loudly, but Donna doesn't believe her.)

Julie hugged him. She had never before appreciated the fact that he did the trash. She never cared before if it was overflowing and she threw one more thing in (and secretly she knew it was her wrapper that missed the can). She will never take *his* job for granted again.

The trick, of course, is to also let him see what *you* do—so he can appreciate it.

> **CORE STRATEGIES FOR SUCCESS:**
> **Prioritize**
> **Eliminate Extraneous Tasks**
> **Negotiate**

We look at the domestic-chore issue from a management perspective: A man and a woman can be equally fantastic managers, but they will probably bring male and female strengths, respectively, to bear upon their jobs. And so it is in the home.

Now, if you know how to rotate the tires on your SUV and your husband can sew a straight hem, excellent: We salute you. But don't beat yourselves up if the household tasks get done according to gender preferences. (Even some of the tasks with the children. We had one friend who divided the baby bodily-fluid responsibilities up along a great divide. She got the South: diapers. He got the North: vomiting. (She's not quite sure why he could better put up with puke than poo, but she thinks it has something to do with all those nights he spent doing beer bongs with his frat brothers.)

So what feats of magic did we perform to get our husbands more amenable to doing stuff around the house? We'd like to tell you there's something we did to make our men go, "Hey, organizing the spice rack? Lemme at it!" but that would be a big ol' lie. Much of what we did was simply managing our own expectations. Instead of coming to our husbands with a list of 100 things that needed to be done yesterday—which was our old approach—we would instead winnow down the list and figure out what was totally unimportant, what we could do ourselves, and what we really needed him to do. This clarifying-and-delegating process was critical in getting our houses to run smoothly again. Here are some of the highlights:

What Actually Happens Around Your House—and What Needs to Happen? Sounds basic, doesn't it? But during the time we were separated, Julie and I realized there were many things our husbands were doing of which we were completely unaware. Julie might be furious that Phillip didn't understand the absolute necessity of sorting socks according to size, color, and wear (nothing's worse than a sock that's newish with a sock that's oldish . . . different levels of fuzziness, ugh ugh ugh). Yet she did not know, until he was no longer home, that every other week Phillip was taking the second propane tank to be filled in case the first one ran out. She had no idea they even had two propane tanks, and, in truth, she had never really thought about how the one she was aware of got filled in the first place.

So before having a sit-down with your husband about

chores, it's good to know what those chores are. He may not be sitting on his butt as much as you think.

Then again, he might.

Negotiate, Negotiate, Negotiate: If you've followed our little formula in the first part of this chapter, you have, we hope, narrowed down your list of domestic responsibilities. If you started with 100 items, eliminated/allocated 50, you've got 50 left. Now let the trading begin.

To ensure the negotiation doesn't devolve into a messy argument, we made the whole thing into a game. It goes like this:

THE "WOULD YOU RATHER" GAME

This is a game that will help your partner become your domestic god. The object is to assign chores but to allow for preferences.

If you and your partner both work full-time, the number of chores should be shared equally.

If one of you works part-time/does not work and the other works full-time, you should prorate the number of chores based on a "full-time work schedule."

Step 1: Make a list of all your household chores and write each one on an index card.

Step 2: Order the chores by amount of time it takes to accomplish each task.

Step 3: Group the chores into the following categories:
  • Greater than 1 hour to accomplish
  • Between 30 minutes and 1 hour
  • Less than 30 minutes

Step 4: Give you and your spouse two jokers from a deck of playing cards. These will be used in the event that a particular chore is something neither of you wants to do.

Step 5: Flip a coin to see who goes first.

Step 6: Turn over two of the index cards from the same category and ask the person who goes first which they'd rather do. The chore they'd rather do goes in their pile.

Step 7: Return the unchosen card to the pile and turn up two new cards, rotate turn, and repeat step 6.

Repeat steps 6 and 7 until all cards are assigned.

If, during play, you decide to use your joker, the partner who plays the card gets to assign the chore to the other rather than returning it to the pile.

(Variation: If you have children old enough to help with chores, you would sort out a few cards into a pile for them, based on age appropriateness. If you have more than one child, you could sort out cards and have them play their own game as described above.)

Once the chores have been divvied up, the goal here is to *set expectations*, and don't let anyone in the family, least of all your husband, have to guess what he has to do. Remember, even though he's going to have some responsibilities that will be his and his alone, it is also very freeing for him to know *there are some things around the house he'll never have to do* (unless, of course, there's some emergency). It can be a huge relief. It's just like having an executive assistant. In a job that involves

many detail-oriented tasks, anything you can do to further define job description (no getting coffee, no picking up my dry
cleaning) often means those tasks that are his and his alone will
be accomplished better and more cheerfully.

So, for example, Donna and Dave came to the the following
arrangement:

Shared responsibilities:

> Buying groceries
> Buying household supplies
> Cooking
> Dish washing
> Housecleaning

Donna's responsibilities:

> Dry cleaning (it's all Donna's anyway, unless she forces
>   Dave to get gussied up)
> Donna's car (although Dave does mechanics if it's
>   something he can fix himself)
> House decorating/furniture (Donna picks it out; he is
>   allowed to veto if he's truly horrified)
> All pet care (dog and Chinese water dragons)

Dave's responsibilities:

> Garbage
> Yard work
> Maintenance of anything that has an On/Off switch

Julie and Phillip's division of labor is quite different—particularly since their gifts do not divide across typical gender lines. As Julie explains:

I am not, strictly speaking, a gourmet cook. What happens, invariably, is that I rethink every ingredient in a recipe. For example: making Thai food one night (correction: TRYING to make Thai food one night): I go to the store with the recipe. I buy the coconut milk. I buy the hot red paste. I see that it calls for fish oil. Hmmm. Fish oil? Why would fish oil be in this? Oh—it's only 1/8 of a teaspoon, what could it possibly add to the flavor? I don't need that. Then the next ingredient . . . sesame oil? Hmmm. That sounds good—oh, it's $9.00 a bottle and I'm only going to make this once. . . . I don't need that. And on and on until really, what I end up with is linguine in a sauce that looks like pink milk and tastes like crap.

The only things I know how to do with ANY talent (other than ordering out, opening containers, or reheating) are boil stuff and sprinkle spices that you can see. So—it's either pasta with sauce for dinner (two ingredients if you don't count the sprinkle cheese that you add on at the end) or anything else with salt, pepper, and oregano—because then it LOOKS like I did something to it because it has all those green flakes. So, gourmet cook? No. Gourmet boiler, spicer, reheater, orderer? Without a doubt.

In an effort not to ever see a bowl of pasta with burnt-stuff-and-oregano on it again, Phillip has become quite a good cook. So when he's home, dinner is ready by the time I get there (or the time I'm supposed to get there). Usually, his schedule only allows that to happen a few days a week. During the day—especially during summer—he cooks for all of us. And he cooks for all the holidays. As Phillip's become more at ease in the kitchen, he takes more pleasure in cooking. And I take great pleasure in watching him and enjoying the fruits of his labor.

Determine Those Tasks That May Be Solved in Ways Other Than "You Do It/I Do It/the Kids Do It": Sometimes, a solution to a domestic squabble can be solved without anyone having to change or compromise.

Julie loves dishes—she'd have a dozen sets, if she could afford them. And although she hasn't had time to give a big party in the last few years, she continues to buy more pieces of her favorite holiday set—although she suspects her new olive plate will never see an olive. Maybe, if she buys enough, somehow the guilt of having all those dishes will *force* her to have a party!

At any rate, everyone in her family is united in their hatred of washing dishes. And Julie realized that the family's endless "who's-doing-the-dishes?" argument, while often solved with Julie's work chart (i.e., everyone does take turns), was still a problem when she and Phillip and the older kids were in the middle of a work crunch. So, while it's not something of which an environmentalist would approve, Julie now keeps a large supply of paper goods—plates, cups, napkins—around the house for those occasions.

Donna, while acknowledging that her need for a neat toothpaste tube does not rank up there with the need for potable water in third world countries, nevertheless would get irked every single time she saw a tube of toothpaste gummed up at the top or squeezed in the middle as if the Incredible Hulk had just dropped by to brush and floss. A few years ago, Mentadent came out with the toothpaste pump dispenser. Donna heard the angels and harp strings: Here was a solution that would get her exactly what she wanted, with no hardship on anyone's part, or indeed the recognition that anything had changed.

Let There Be Consequences: If a designated task is not done, let it stay undone. Don't swoop in and make everything right. (Well, if something left undone poses an actual health hazard, you'll want to reconsider. If a raccoon wanders into the living room, maybe it's in your interest to shoo it out, even if pest control is His Job.) Maybe this means that you will be living without Cheerios for a few days, or that the level of dog hair on the furniture reaches critical mass. Allow the evildoer to incur the wrath not of you but of the kids. This tactic takes a certain amount of forebearance on your part. Can you be cheerful in the face of a huge pile of unironed laundry? Well, learn to be, because remember this: *If you continually solve a problem that is not yours, you have created a new, more difficult problem.*

Motivate, Motivate Motivate: We've talked repeatedly and in many contexts about the importance of positive reinforcement, and that reinforcement may be particularly important here, in the land of Annoying Chores Only a Mental Patient Could Truly Enjoy. (Well, mental patients and Julie. Really, if we could, we would have included a photo of her sock drawer.)

Anyone looking for ways to motivate her mate could take a few lessons from the people who design sales incentive packages. The underlying idea behind incentive compensation programs is called the *Expectancy Theory*, which can be summed up in four steps:

Effort, which leads to
Performance, which leads to
Reward (or **Punishment**, if the performance is poor)
  which leads to
Satisfaction (or **Dissatisfaction**, if there is a
  punishment).

The Expectancy Theory asks a business manager three questions:

1. Will effort lead to performance? That's **Expectancy**.
2. Does performance lead to reward? That's
   Instrumentality. Instrumentality is the employees'
   confidence that management will honor its promises.
3. Do I value the reward? That's called **Valence**. Valence
   refers to the emotional expectations people hold with
   respect to outcomes, that is, the depth of a person's
   desires for extrinsic (money, promotion, time off,
   benefits) or intrinsic (satisfaction at a job well done)
   rewards. Valence can be plus, minus, or zero.

If the answer is "no" to any question, motivation is **zero**. So there has to be a clear "yes" answer to each question, in order for a person to be motivated.

The most important aspects of motivating your man are threefold:

1. *Expectations must be defined:* He has to know exactly
   what you want. And no, "If he really loved me he'd
   know what I wanted" is WRONG. Guesswork is not
   allowed.

2. *The reward has to be desirable.* Saying that if he spends all day with the children, you are going to take him out to see *Terms of Endearment*? Not going to help your cause. Taking him out to see Jessica Simpson starring in *Lethal Weapon XI: The Rapture*? Helpful.

3. *The valued reward has to be* guaranteed *if the desired goal is reached.* In other words, if he has a 100-percent chance of getting laid after sitting through the anniversary dinner of wacky Uncle Phil and Aunt Betty, the ones who raise Pekingese dogs, he will be a gracious and charming guest. If you make the promise but add the caveat that you're beginning to feel your fibromyalgia acting up . . . his charm will be in short supply. *Uncertainty undermines motivation.*

Outsource What You Can: Maybe your budget simply doesn't allow for help. That's fine. But if you and your husband are fighting constantly about who cleans what . . . consider the possibility that one less article of clothing per month, one or two fewer meals out, would pay for a once-a-week or once-every-two-weeks housekeeper and could drastically cut down on fighting.

A few nights ago, Donna came home late after a particularly brutal day. She arrived home to find the groceries bought, a grilled chicken and trimmings ready, a bouquet of fresh flowers on the table, and the children post-bath, all clean and shiny. She asked Dave what was up; he said, "Nothing. Just loving you." Not every night is like this, for sure. But it was a scene that was unimaginable two years ago.

Incentive plans work. Later that night, Dave got his reward. A reward for both, really.

CHAPTER 8

Plan

Become Fiscally Responsible

• • • •

> Men might as well be imprisoned, as excluded
> from the means of earning their bread.
>
> —JOHN STUART MILL

A friend of ours is a female CEO of a major company whose longtime boyfriend makes about $75,000 a year. For most of us this is a fine salary; to the CEO, it's her expense account for lunch. Yet this man pays his share of the rent; he bought his own car; he sent his children (from a previous marriage) through college by taking out loans. True, he gets to drive her Porsche and live in her beachfront house in Malibu. But the CEO won't pay a dime toward most of his living expenses. Despite the fact that she loves him, and can certainly afford to give him anything, she lives in fear of becoming that most pathetic of women: the one whose lover sponges off her.

Is she a bitch? Is she a pragmatist? You decide. One thing is certain: She might be making millions, but she needed at least the illusion of being cared for. Call it being a tightwad. Or call it being female.

It seems the female brain is hardwired to demand that a man bring home something. Not a lot, *something*. In fact, whatever our relative incomes, many women feel uncomfortable defining themselves as "the breadwinner." In 1997, sociologist Jean L. Potuchek, an associate professor in the women's studies department at Gettysburg College, interviewed 153 randomly chosen couples where both husband and wife were working. Potuchek learned that only 15 percent of wives and 26 percent of husbands reported that they fully shared responsibility for breadwinning—even though, with all these couples, family finances were their primary motivation for employment, and the wives' jobs accounted for a substantial portion of the family income. It was a question of definition—both men and women agreed that the men were the "breadwinners," regardless of who actually made the most money. Said Potuchek, "Americans value differences between men and women and act to highlight those differences in their daily lives through the creation of gender boundaries."

So that's the attitude we, as a culture, live with. Women can earn the bucks, but we don't usually define ourselves as breadwinners—because somehow that is stripping our men of their masculinity. While this isn't always the case, we do agree that women possess a deep-seated need to have the men in their lives be serious about money, no matter who earns it.

Women are also frequently accused of being too conservative with money—but there may be a good reason for that, too. According to one recent study, husbands tend to suffer a bit of irrational exuberance when it comes to the family finances. A 2003 nationwide study at Ohio University asked 1,195 couples about the family finances, and typically the husband says the couple earns 5 percent more income and has 10 percent more total wealth than the wife reports. The majority of husbands also reported they made more money than they actually did, and their wives made less than they actually did, whatever the truth of the situation. (The researchers did not check to see the truth of the couple's finances—only the perception.) And it's not that the wives were ill-informed. Both husbands and wives agreed that husbands tended to pay the bills around 40 percent of the time, and wives around 60 percent of the time. It doesn't take much extrapolation from this study to see why, in many households, the husband and wife are like the grasshopper and the ant: The grasshopper/husband lives for the moment, and the ant/wife wants to "save for a rainy day."

OUR SCORECARD FOR FISCAL RESPONSIBILITY

- **Share responsibility for paying bills**
- **Help with tax filings and payments**
- **Stop paying ATM fees**
- **Set priorities and take care of financial obligations before buying luxuries**
- **Discuss and agree on discretionary spending with your partner**
- **Help plan family vacations**
- **Help plan holiday travel**
- **Create a joint savings plan**
- **Establish financial goals together**
- **Create a pay-off-debt plan**
- **Start a college savings plan**
- **Start a retirement plan**
- **Establish an organized approach for record keeping**
- **Help determine and work toward long-term family goals**
- **Participate in insurance decisions**

· **Help decide investment planning and strategy**
· **Participate in drafting a will**

....

✳ Money, Honey: ✳
Your Scorecard

STEP ONE—Prioritize: List all the ways you want your partner to be more fiscally responsible—thinking about the family not just today but in the future. Fill them in on their proper places on your four-block chart, identifying which items are of highest priority for you. Our four-block looked like this:

✳ **OUR RELATIONSHIP MAP: FISCAL RESPONSIBILITY** ✳	
ND • Participate in insurance decisions • Help decide investment planning and strategy • Participate in drafting a will	**ID** • Stop paying ATM fees • Set priorities and take care of financial obligations before buying luxuries • Discuss and agree on discretionary spending with your partner • Share responsibility for paying bills • Help with tax filings and payments • Create a joint savings plan • Establish financial goals together • Pay-off-debt plan • Help determine and work toward long-term family goals
NS • Create organized approach for record keeping • Help plan holiday travel • Help plan family vacations	**IS** • Create college savings plan • Create retirement plan

(vertical axis label) **LEVEL OF DISSATISFACTION**

IMPORTANCE

STEP TWO—Filter: Take the items in the upper right quadrant of your four-block—the items of highest importance and greatest dissatisfaction.

For each item, ask:

- Is there a one-time fix to this issue (that is, get rid of all but one credit card, cut up the ATM card, get a cheaper cell-phone plan)?
- Can I fix this with technology or a new product that is on the market? (Hello, TurboTax!)

These are the items you can handle. Set them aside. For all others in the right-hand quadrant, continue to step three.

STEP THREE—Analyze: For items that remain, you'll need to develop an approach to fixing them. Determine whether an item is going to be easy or hard to fix by asking yourself the following questions:

- Is my husband going to be cooperative on this issue? (There are some issues that might be solved by a well-planned conversation, but others where you know that your partner will be entrenched in his point of view, custom, or cultural perspective.)
- Do we (my husband or I) have the skills necessary to properly address this issue?
- Has this been an issue for less than one year?
- Can the task be done by only one person?

If you answered "yes" to all of these—we would call your problem easy. If you answered "no" to any of the questions—your problem would be considered hard.

For Easy Problems: We recommend approaching your husband with a recommendation and a quick conversation. He may be unaware, for example, that keeping most of his money in a checking account, with zero interest, is a very bad idea. Just because he's not a financial whiz doesn't mean he's not open to suggestions.

For Hard Problems: We recommend that if your husband isn't cooperative, prep work may be needed in order to gain agreement or compliance. If neither of you has the skill set, you may need to go to training or pay someone else to do it (lawyer, financial planner, or accountant).

STEP FOUR—Plan Your Approach: When Dave and Donna got back together after their separation, there wasn't that much negotiating about who would pay what; Donna, being the larger earner, had no problem paying the major bills like mortgage and school costs, and Dave, the smaller earner, would pay day-to-day things like gas and cable. Donna hated paying bills; Dave enjoyed it. Every month they deposited a set amount of money for monthly expenses in a checking account. Donna made sure her bills were sent directly from the account, while David organized and paid his bills by hand. There was both accountability and a means of being financially responsible. They embraced their strengths and worked around their weaknesses.

> ### CORE STRATEGIES FOR SUCCESS:
> #### Shared Accountability
> #### Support/Praise/Cheerleading to Gain Compliance
> #### Goal Setting
> #### Team Building

Neither Donna nor Julie live lavishly, or aspire to live lavishly. (Julie is in the middle of putting an addition onto a modest Cape Cod-style home in Chicago, and Donna lives in a small rectangular ranch house that . . . well, if it had wheels, it could be a double-wide at any moment.) But they have vastly different money styles, which meant their financial lives went south in different ways.

Donna, for example, doesn't keep careful track of her money, which meant that when Dave snuck out a little bit here and a little bit there—you need constant cash on hand when you're out in the middle of the night buying bar rounds for your buddies—it took her a while to notice. The overdraft notices piled up. And then she was forced to do an audit of her accounts—which really infuriated her, because there's nothing she hates more than this kind of scrutinizing. In the end she was forced to play Mommy, taking away Dave's bank card and cutting off all access to cash. Which—surprise!—only made him sneakier. Her beloved (and normally very honest) husband became an excellent thief.

Julie checks over her accounts carefully, yet she hadn't thought through their new situation. When she and Phillip moved to Chicago from New Jersey for a new, much-higher-paying salary, Julie thought she was finally raking in the big bucks. She failed to account for the fact that though her wages had doubled, her cost of living had tripled. And her resentment piled up as she worked harder and harder and her husband stayed home, did nothing, and spent money ever more frivolously. Julie's particular *bête noire* was the amount Phillip spent on ATM fees. He'd stop and take out $20 a day and pay a $2 fee each time. She continually tried to explain to him that a tiny amount of planning would eliminate the 10 percent charge he was wasting on all their discretionary spending cash. At some point she gave Phillip an ultimatum: Stop doing this or get a separate account. Finally—when he didn't change—Julie sliced up his ATM card with a pair of scissors and made him get a separate account. It wasn't just the $2 fee; it was what that fee said about Phillip's carelessness toward his family.

Neither of us cared that we made more than our husbands. And when they said they wanted to be stay-at-home fathers (even if it was just while they did a "soft" job search), that was a great contribution. There was only one problem: Ultimately, despite their best intentions, they weren't equipped for the job. It isolated and depressed them, just as it isolates and depresses many women. Only for them it was worse, because they did not have the social approbation that stay-at-home mothers do. These were guy's guys, used to the company of men. After a while, both felt someone had slapped a giant LOSER sticker on their foreheads with Krazy Glue, and they would have ripped their skin off to remove it.

Ironically, too, our own Wonder Woman complexes tripped us up. Our husbands thought we were so competent that there was no way we would need them financially. Whatever contribution they made . . . well, it was "play money." In effect, our strength and independence gave them license to be spendthrifts.

As we've discussed throughout the book, our (sometimes very tough) job was to stop enabling irresponsible behavior—and as we've also said repeatedly, you don't have to throw your husband out the door to accomplish the same goal. Whether he's a stay-at-home dad, or you stay at home with the kids, or you both work full-time, the bottom line is that you have to be clear and direct; and you need a plan. Nowhere is this more true than in the arena of money, which, in survey after survey, is at the top of the list of "Things We Fight About" among couples.

Here are the strategies that worked for us:

Before You Talk Dollars, Learn to Talk Sense: Planning an Effective Discussion: It can be excruciating to discuss something as sensitive as money. However, there are ways you can prepare yourself to have a more successful discussion and get the outcome you want. The key is planning.

1. Define the issue or concern (the topic of the discussion).

   Example—"I'd like my husband to be more mindful of how we spend money on the children."

2. Add details to explain exactly what you mean.

   Example—We're at a point where we need to start making plans for our kids' education, and instead he always goes for the short-term gratification: the new DVD, the tenth pair of jeans. Life seems to be about just making today pleasant, without giving any real thought to their future. Because of this, I'm anxious all the time.

Here, you are stating the purpose, importance, and impact of the issue.

3. Identify what's in it for him.

Example—Security; knowing your kids will be grateful to you; knowing they'll have the kind of chances they deserve—perhaps the kind of education *you* (or he) deserved and didn't have.

4. Ask for his involvement in finding ways to solve the problem before presenting your own ideas, and then share your ideas.

5. Agree on a plan of action.

Example—This Friday, we'll go to the bank and open a 529 college savings account.

DISCUSSION-PLANNING TEMPLATE

(Note: Here, we're talking about money and planning for the future. But, in fact, the discussion planner can apply to any sensitive, hard-to-bring-up topic.)

Define the issue

_____

_____

_____

Details: purpose, importance, impact

_____

_____

_____

What's in it for him? Why should he care?

Ideas (yours and his)

Actions

Let Your "Money Styles" Determine How You Handle the Family Finances in General: It's wonderful if you and your husband have the same approach to money. You both have your beloved Quicken for doing taxes—or, alternatively, you both tell yourselves you can keep lots of numbers in your head and don't need all that fancy-schmancy software. When someone offers you a "hot" stock tip, you both jump on it—or you both do research; you both obsessively bargain hunt—or you both shop at Prada; you both think daily about your financial future—or it never crosses your minds. That is financial harmony.

But most of us live with considerably more discord. It's amazing how many of us who are methodical about gaining financial knowledge live with people who, when asked how they make a financial decision, say proudly, "I go with my gut."

So if it's all-too-clear to you that he's a spender and you're a saver, or vice versa, fine; it may be better for you to keep separate accounts. There used to be something of a stigma attached to the married couple who did this—what, don't they trust each other?—but apparently those days are gone. In 2004, the Raddon Financial Group, a research company, surveyed 1,200 couples nationwide and found that fully 48 percent of them kept separate accounts. Usually, the reason cited was that people spend money differently, but sometimes it was because one person in the couple had a bad credit rating, or one partner wanted to reserve money to benefit children from a previous marriage.

We both realized that joint accounts were a mistake for us. Now, with separate accounts, as long as each partner fulfills his or her responsibilities to the household every month, neither is looking over the other's shoulder to see where every last penny goes.

You may decide to create a separate account for family expenses, or you may do something like what Donna and Dave do—just assign certain expenses to each spouse, according to your own idea of fairness. (In their case, where Donna makes about three times what her husband makes, she pays mortgage, insurance [home and auto], and child care, which are their biggest drain, and Dave has all of the other expenses: cable, gas, electric, water, and phone. He makes his own car payment, Donna makes hers, and they each cover their own credit card payments.

The structure Julie and Phillip worked out to determine contribution is quite simple. As much as possible we take the financial doings of the household out of the emotional realm (we know: tough), and try to stick to a businesslike proposition.

- Evaluate Income: What's the total family income? You include everything from monthly paychecks to money realized from stock trades to under-the-table tips. Everything needs to be be accounted for, and a percentage set aside for something other than buying the latest iPod. Also, are there any bonuses, raises, or other income that may come in that should be taken into account?

- Let's say, for the sake of argument, that total family income is $5,000 a month.
- Determine Expenses: How much is leaving the household, more or less, on basic, can't-be-avoided bills? (Let's say, $4,800 a month.)
- Categorize Current Spending: Is most of the money going toward utilities, groceries, insurance, clothing, gas, etc.? Discuss whether or not these expenditures seem to be in line with everyone's expectations. ($2,000 a month for rent, $1,000 for other utilities, $600 for groceries, etc.). There are some expenses our husbands paid entirely on their own, and some we did. (We didn't need to pay for their cars, and they didn't need to pay for our hair highlights.)
- How Much Is Left Over? If there is anything left, how is it being spent? Savings for the future (retirement/college), vacation savings, holiday gifts? Does it just stay in the account until there's a big expense? (Let's say $200 goes into a savings account.)

From here, the real discussion begins. (In this case: Why in God's name are we saving only $200 a month?! We need to save $500 a month for this year's vacation! etc., etc.) For Phillip and Julie, as for so many Americans, their most difficult problem was getting themselves out from under the masses of credit card debt that they had accumulated since they moved to Chicago. What good is saving money at 5–8 percent a year if you have a credit card debt of 15–20 percent?

Big shocker: Both Donna and Julie are still the major savers, since they make more money. And they do the family taxes because, let's face it, if their husbands did them they would all end up in jail.

What's important, of course, are not the details of the financial system you and your husband have in place but the very fact that you agree on the system you have, and that you've put at least the bare bones of a system into place (although Julie would be thrilled to discuss with you the details of her debt-consolidation strategy, 401(k), and tax filings going back fifteen years). It's never been about the dollar amount their husbands can contribute. It's that Dave and Phillip have gone from thinking first about their own needs to thinking about the family's needs. As Donna explains:

> *Initially, there was a lot of resistance to having a codified financial arrangement in place between me and Dave. To me, the pragmatist, it seemed perfectly normal; to Dave, the romantic, it seemed weird and overly businesslike between a married couple. He'd say to me, "Why do I have to follow your rules?" To which I would answer, "You don't! Make up your own rules, and let's talk about them. But we need to have SOME rules in place in order to have a life together that works. If you want to set the agenda, do it—don't just sit back and complain.*

At first, Julie's negotiations with Phillip were similarly fraught:

I don't think everything clicked for Phillip until he was responsible for the input, the output, AND the debt payments. There was a time when he would just make money and it went into a big pot. Then I would pay the bills and he had no idea what/who we owed. At one time we owed MAJOR credit card debt. MAJOR. You would GASP. We reached an initial agreement on how much he would give me each month to contribute toward the family expenses and he gives me a check each time he gets paid. Occasionally, when he wants to make a large purchase that will increase the family debt, this requires a "renegotiation" of the former arrangement. When we have our "renegotiations" there are all these financial trade-offs that we do, but he is VERY cognizant of our debt situation now. For example, one trade-off involved a new television Phillip wanted. My perspective was that it was something that should come out of disposable income—and there wasn't a similar big-ticket item that I wanted, so it wasn't equitable. But we worked it out. He got the TV and I ended up getting a larger pro-rata share of his paychecks so when I paid down the family debt, he was paying his fair share.

Start Small (Maybe Really, Really Small): If you're married to someone who feels about finances as meteorologists feel about global warming, then you've got to respect his limitations—and work with them. This means that you don't start with "Honey, how much money will we need for the future so we're not eating cat food when we're sixty-five?" Instead, think about putting him in charge of the small stuff: setting the kids' allowances, budgeting the Christmas party, perhaps paying the bills online (so he doesn't really have to balance the checkbook—it's sort of balanced for him). He's never going to become Warren Buffett, but at least he'll feel more at ease than he does now.

Take a Rational, Nonemotional Approach to Discretionary Spending:
Wouldn't it be fabulous if you and your partner had the same priorities, tastes, and preferences for nonessential household items? That you never had to argue about which you needed most—the cappuccino maker or the humidor? But chances are you don't. So how do you determine how to spend your discretionary funds? What gets the thumbs-up: the TiVo you want to record shows while at work or the $4,000 Bose Home Entertainment System that automatically organizes 340 hours of digital music and insures your husband will not leave his La-Z-Boy for three months?

Here's a strategy we've developed to help you stop fighting about which extras are the most important. (P.S.: We only go through this exercise with items above a certain dollar threshold. For us, it's $500; you may find another number, higher or lower, works better for you.) The object here is to create **one** list that prioritizes what you will purchase with your discretionary funds.

1. You and your husband each make a list of what you would buy.
2. Order those items by preference/priority.
3. Next, figure out a way to decide who gets to go first. (A coin toss might work, though we do three rounds of rock/paper/scissors and the best two out of three wins.)

Whoever wins gets to put their preferred item first on the shared list as #1. Alternate back and forth through your lists until you have consolidated the list, 1,2,3,4,5 . . .

Do some of your partner's items scare you? The bronze bust of Hockey Hall of Famer Bobby Hull? If you think there will be items that you absolutely cannot live with, you might think about using the trump-card approach: Each of you gets one trump card you can use to veto your partner's most objectionable item.

Over time, you may want to add, delete, or prioritize. Each person may substitute something on the shared list, but if you add something, you need to either put it at the bottom of the list or move an item you replace with the new item to the bottom of the list.

Start Thinking About the Far-off Future by Being Mindful of the Near Future: If you were an alien who landed on Earth and started paying attention to popular culture, you'd get one overarching idea about the human race: The young have all the fun. More to the point, they are the ones who feel more intensely, who live life at a faster clip, who are in general more passionate and emotional.

In fact, the very opposite is true. Solid research has shown that our emotions become more intense and complex as we age. Why? Is it the wisdom gained with the gathering years? A shift in values thanks to greater life experience? Not really. Rather, it has to do with a keener sense of time—a precious and diminishing resource. One recent test of this idea at the University of California, San Diego, asked 165 young subjects—average age twenty years—to imagine themselves in several different scenarios. Half were told to imagine "limited future" scenarios, such as the last day of a holiday. The other half were not asked to consider the future at all. Then they were all asked to rate the intensity of a variety of emotions to the occasion. "Given time limits, people showed more extreme emotions—on both the positive and negative ends of the scale," said the lead researcher, Ursina Teuscher. "The test results suggest that a different time perspective itself can cause differences in emotional complexity and intensity."

This quirk of human nature goes a long way to explaining why decisions about the future together become so fraught. Planning for the future forces you to look not at the quotidian (*How can I make sure my kids aren't late for school every day?*) but at the emotionally rich, sometimes satisfying, sometimes nerve-racking Big Picture. *How much time do we have to save for college? How much time do we have for us when the kids are gone? HOW MUCH TIME DO WE HAVE?* Thinking far in advance brings up questions of mortality—and who wants to think about *that?* We have friends for whom planning-for-the-future discussions ushered in full-blown midlife crises in their mates. Well, OK, maybe not full-blown—they didn't leave their wives for nineteen-year-olds—but instead of soberly considering the future, the message they got was *Life is short, I need to buy that thirty-foot sloop right now.*

You never can be sure how your own husband will react, of course. But you have a much better chance of planning calmly for the far-off future if you get him in the habit of being mindful of the *near* future. What do we mean by this? Well, it is the rare couple, used to living life in the here and now, who can then make the big leap to doing things like setting up a 401(k), 529 college funds, and preparing wills. Take the interim step: If you know how to plan for next week, or a month from now, you're more likely to look further off into the future, too.

This is why, for example, Julie keeps a Family Communication Board in the dining room of her house. Anything important related to the family goes on this board, since she and Phillip discovered that telling each other about an event a week in the future is one thing—remembering it is another. The board looks like this:

1. Calendar (with days when Phillip needs the nanny to stay late/come early, kids' days off from school, important events, trips, etc.)
2. Birthday list
3. Chores list
4. Grocery/shopping lists
5. Important phone numbers and any doctor's appointment cards/reminders
6. NEW THIS MONTH! (which might be, say, Phil's American Express receipts in an envelope)
7. Any random communication among the family. . . . Madelyn put up a birthday invitation to remind Julie to buy a gift; Lauren may put up a coupon to a good restaurant (she knows that it's more likely Julie will take her if there's a discount); Phillip's biweekly check; requests for help on small issues Julie doesn't want to deal with (the please-send-the-thank-you-for-the-baby-present-your-boss's-wife-sent kind of notes).

To us, the ability to look forward is simply a matter of creating a habit. If you can think about what you're doing as a family next month or next holiday season, it's not such a huge leap to a year, five years, or even ten years from now.

Don't Dismiss His Fears or Reluctance: Sometimes, you want your husband to do something he genuinely may not know how to do, or where he needs some assistance. This is true in every arena, of course, but when it comes to money issues you may need to exercise particular sensitivity. After all, this is supposed to be "his" area. Most men we know are as eager to ask for help in managing finances as they are to ask directions: There's just something hardwired that tells them "This is something I should know"; "this is something I'm expected to be competent at"—*for no apparent reason.*

So if he does express his fears to you, don't pooh-pooh them. It's far better to be with a man who will admit ignorance in financial matters than one who boldly goes ahead and makes all sorts of plans that ultimately tank.

And if your level of knowledge and expertise is as limited as his—*admit it.* We sometimes had a hard time admitting we knew nothing about a subject, particularly when our husbands were used to seeing us as so competent and all-knowing. We liked that version of ourselves! We didn't want to blow it! But at the same time, it was in no one's interest to pretend to be a know-it-all about something as important as the family's financial future. *It's important to be a role model for your husband by seeking help when you need it.*

Get Him Used to Thinking, We, Not I: This is the essence of team-building. At work, teams often feel closer when they accomplish goals together. We aren't suggesting the family sets out to build a bridge together with newspaper or tries to overcome an obstacle course like some of the corporate team-building gurus may suggest, but we do think that as you accomplish smaller goals on the list, you will feel more momentum toward the larger items. Pick a few small goals and target those first. It's hard to believe, but when you feel like you have common goals, the world is suddenly US versus THEM and not ME versus YOU. If you've ever been in any competitive business situation, you know exactly what we're talking about here. Husbands and wives are no different.

There are a variety of places where this approach works, from housework to vacation planning, to managing the sometimes-conflicting schedules of your children.

From a vacation-planning perspective, Donna and Julie are fortunate working for United Airlines, so it's not too tough to get travel information. Donna and Dave involve their children in selecting vacation spots and divvying up the planning. Dave is a planner, which Donna leverages by having him map out what they're going to do and organizing the agenda.

Create the Financial Planning Infrastructure, Even If You Don't Have the Funds to Pour Into It Yet: What this means is: Research the life insurance you want, open up the special account earmarked for your big ten-year-anniversary getaway, do the paperwork to get the children's (tax-deferred) 529 college funds in place. It's extremely important to lay all the groundwork, even if you don't have much money yet available to throw in the direction of these projects. It's the same principle you'd use on little kids: They're not going to save money if they don't have the piggy bank to put it in.

These discussions can also be a great filtering point for discretionary spending items. If you have a list of investments you want to build, when you have discretionary items come up for discussion, you can bounce them off your investments list to check where it makes most sense to spend your money: Is it time to purchase the entertainment system or should we shift that expenditure into the college savings account?

Money 101: For all sorts of money-planning issues, http://moneycentral.msn.com is a great place to start. Banking, investing, planning, taxes, real estate, insurance, and loan information: It's all here, with links to scores of other sites. This being a Microsoft site, there's plenty of shilling for software programs like MSN Money (which helps you control your financial life—viewing bank statements, consolidating views of your accounts, tracking spending by category, forecasting cash flow, creating reports about your spending habits, managing upcoming and unpaid bills—from one central location). But there are also many free and useful articles, plus tools and calculators for every conceivable financial challenge you face.

For College: www.savingforcollege.com is an excellent site that will tell you everything you need to know about socking away enough money so you won't have an aneurysm when faced with that first tuition bill. The site lays out the pros and cons of various savings strategies, but its emphasis is on the relatively new 529 plans available in every state—how much you can put away tax-deferred, how much grandparents can give, what happens if your child doesn't go to college, and so forth—and explains why these relatively new programs are so popular. (Basically, the money is still in your control; you're not handing it over to your child. Which means Timmy can't decide, at sixteen, that the college savings plan would be much better spent on a Ferrari.)

For information comparing the success of individual plans in recent years you'd have to become a member of savingfor college.com—but in fact that information is also available in newspaper articles on the subject. The site includes a college calculator, which allowed us to figure out that even though we were putting away about $5,000 per year per child, we needed to put away a couple of thousand more to meet the costs for the most expensive colleges, if we enrolled in a moderately aggressive savings plan.

So, in conclusion, the upside of www.savingforcollege.com: solid information. The downside: mild panic.

Saving for Retirement: For information about retirement plans, we like www.retireplan.about.com and money.cnn.com/retirement/. One of the best things about retireplan.about.com is that it offers a glossary of terms like 401 (k) and 403 (b) and . . . well, let's put it this way: FINALLY, we were clued in to exactly what an annuity really is: "Tax favored investments that allow you to make a series of fixed amount payments at regular intervals over the period of the annuity. These investments then generate a series of regular payments guaranteed to continue for a specific time."

OK, maybe you knew this. We didn't—not exactly. There comes a time in your life when you throw around financial terms willy-nilly, because you're a little embarrassed to admit you don't know exactly what they mean. Or they've been explained to you a dozen times, but still, every time they're explained, your eyes glaze over. So that's why we love this site.

We'll never have to ask anyone to explain a Keogh plan to us again.

Stock Advice: Most of us do not have the trust in a money manager to turn over all money-making decisions, no questions asked. (Or we don't have a hefty-enough portfolio: Most money managers have a minimum dollar amount they work with.) You may have a broker, but you may also want to trade on your own, or at least have input into what your broker is buying and selling for you. For that, Jim Cramer's www.thestreet.com is still the gold standard of stock-trading advice and information. There's the free site, of course, and there are many levels of subscription for the individual investor and the professional trader and areas of the site on particular areas of interest. For example, subscription to realmoney.com provides investment and trading ideas, individual company analysis, and access to the opinions and strategies of some leading Wall Street traders. There are special subscriptions to telecom stocks, dividend stocks, and a host of others.

Estate Planning: We're not suggesting you plan your estate via the Internet unless it's the most straightforward planning possible. But if there's nothing too Byzantine about your plans (you're leaving everything to a spouse, you want a simple declaration of your wishes in case of a catastrophic accident that requires life support) you might want to check out a site like www.legacywriter.com, which, for nominal sums, provides you with the appropriate documentation for wills, living wills, power of attorney, and medical power of attorney. The documents are individualized for whatever state you're living in.

(Each state, for example, has slightly different laws about wills. The only state for which will documentation is not included is Louisiana.)

Don't Forget to Heap on the Praise: The surest way to encourage his involvement in your own financial future is constant approbation and praise. Many of us, both men and women, find it difficult to look at our finances squarely. We'd rather not know exactly what we have or don't have; it's anxiety-provoking and rather dreary, because it forces us to be adults. So the more you make it clear to your husband that he is a superstar, and there is no financial hurdle you can't tackle if you do it together . . . the more he's going to get behind you in your quest to make your family safe and solvent.

Evaluate Your Goals Regularly, But Not Compulsively: In an HR department, you don't whip out a person's performance evaluations every day; rather, you look at performance over a specified period of time, allowing for good patches and bad patches. So you may not want to look at progress in your planning-for-the-future on a monthly basis, but, say, on a quarterly or half-yearly basis—long enough between conversations to regulate progess without panicking if this month or this week there wasn't a penny saved or a long-range plan addressed.

Stop Being Sicilian: You know the old joke about Sicilians . . . how they can never forget a slight? Well, that was us. We carried grudges around like rabbits' feet, pulling them out every now and then to caress lovingly. We never let go.

Phillip and Julie have at least one strong point they both

agree on. No one can bring up old baggage from before they moved into the new house. Their new house meant starting with a clean slate. Period.

So if you're planning for the future, you've both got to learn to let it all go; when you say you forgive, you must actually forgive. (We thought of it as going from being Sicilian to being British: *Fight? What fight? Be a dear and get me another Pim's, would you?*)

One night recently, Julie and Phillip were at the movies, and she had a flashback to the night when their fight about buying the $8 tub of popcorn (why couldn't they have snuck in their own popcorn for fifty cents?) escalated into a referendum about Phillip's wastrel habits. But this night, Julie said nothing and allowed Phillip to buy the $8 popcorn. In fairness, about half the time Phillip makes it himself these days. But Julie has also accepted the fact that to Phillip there is something uniquely satisfying about the taste of overpriced popcorn in a movie theater.

All Hail the Internet. Ten years ago, financial information that was available only to those who could afford a financial advisor, or spend hours logging in time in arcane journals in the library, is now accessible to anyone with a computer and an Internet connection. Of course, big-ticket issues like estate planning and choosing the best retirement savings account may still necessitate talking to a living, breathing professional. But the sites we mentioned can help you get started, and sometimes, can give you the information you need without consulting a lawyer or financial planner.

. . .

What helped both of us enormously in looking toward the future with our husbands was realizing that we were not trying to reclaim the person we married. Instead, we were falling in love with this new creature, one who had fallen and risen again and was shaped by a new set of experiences and values. We could face all those niggling logistical questions about our future lives together because we had let go of the grudges and assumptions of the past. In some ways our relationships felt fresh, because we were with new people—people we could look toward the future with, without fretting about the past.

CHAPTER 9

Evolve

Become the Man You Want to Be

• • • • •

Everyone thinks of changing the world,
but no one thinks of changing himself.

—LEO TOLSTOY

Ever make a New Year's resolution? Nearly one of every two American adults does. And after six months, less than half of those resolutions are carried through.

With the best of intentions, change is tough. And perhaps it's even tougher for men, who often are told from an early age that change is a sign of weakness. One only has to think of the motto "Stay the course"—in the extreme, some have "stayed" no matter how much trouble that course gets them into.

We think that "staying the course" in the face of failure—well, *that's* weakness. And our husbands were anything but weak.

Phillip and Dave set out to change their lives, and they did. Although we joke about how good we are at "fixing" men, the truth is we could not fix them; we could only modify our behavior and interactions with them in a way that would allow them to fix themselves.

OUR SCORECARD FOR PERSONAL GROWTH

....

- Be honest with yourself
- Stop blaming others for your unhappiness
- Reevaluate your spiritual or religious life
- Don't self-medicate with drugs or alcohol
- Stop smoking
- Exercise more
- Take responsibility for your own happiness
- Get into therapy and stay with it
- Confront difficult issues; NO MORE DENIAL
- Manage mental health benefits and filings under your benefits plan
- Get appropriate medication for depression or anxiety, if necessary

....

✳ "Help Me Help You": ✳
Your Scorecard for *His* Growth

STEP ONE—Prioritize: List all the ways you'd like your husband to feel better, look better, think better—*for himself.* Fill them in on their proper places on your four-block chart, identifying which items are of highest priority for you.

⁎ OUR RELATIONSHIP MAP: PERSONAL GROWTH ⁎	
ND • Manage mental health benefits and filings under your benefits plan	**ID** • Find a therapist • Get into therapy and stay with it • Confront difficult issues • Get appropriate medication for depression or anxiety • Be honest with yourself • Stop blaming others for your unhappiness • Don't self-medicate with drugs or alcohol • Stop smoking • Take responsibility for your own happiness
NS • Reevaluate your spiritual or religious life	**IS** • Exercise more

(vertical axis) **LEVEL OF DISSATISFACTION**

IMPORTANCE

STEP TWO—Filter: Take the items in the upper right quadrant of your four-block—the items of highest importance and greatest dissatisfaction.

At this point in each chapter we've been asking, "Is there a one-time fix to such-and-such a problem?" and "Can I fix it with technology or a new product on the market?" Here, of course, there are no "one-time fixes" or quick fixes with new products. This is the one chapter where YOU CANNOT FIX ANYTHING. This is about him.

STEP THREE—Analyze: For all items on the chart that are important, you'll need to develop an approach to *his* fixing them. Determine whether an item is going to be easy or hard to fix by asking yourself the following questions:

- Is my husband going to be cooperative on this issue? (There are some issues that might be solved by a well-planned conversation, but others where you know that your partner will be entrenched in his point of view, custom, or cultural perspective.)
- Does my husband have the skills necessary to properly address this issue?
- Has this been an issue for less than one year?
- Can the task be done by only one person?

If you answered "yes" to all of these—we would call your problem easy. If you answered "no" to any of the questions—your problem would be considered hard.

For Easy Problems: We recommend approaching your husband with a quick conversation. (Maybe, for example, your husband isn't averse to medication but hasn't considered that his depression can be helped pharmacologically. If he's not resistant, it's not difficult to introduce the idea.)

For Hard Problems: We recommend that if your husband isn't sure what direction to take, he may need to go to training or pay someone else to do it (psychologist, spiritual adviser, or life coach).

STEP FOUR—Plan Your Approach: *This is not where we tell you how to solve your husband's problems. This chapter is not about your solving anything. It's about your supporting him as he figures out how to become the man he can be.*

The risk of encouraging your husband to evolve and be honest with himself about his own needs is that he may evolve right out of your life. It's something for which you have to be prepared. But it is also very possible he will evolve back into your life—and your heart.

While you can't change anyone, we do think there are ways you can support a man on his own journey of change. This is what worked in our situations.

Give Him the Benefit of the Doubt: Here is something our combined twenty-five years in management has taught us: Nobody wants to suck at their job. Really. There are very few people who walk into the office and decide, "I'm going to make a mess of things today!" Now, as a manager you figure out there may be many reasons why employees *do* suck: They don't like the work, they lack desire, they do not have the appropriate training, the goals of their position are not clear to them, they have bad interpersonal skills. But you'd be amazed at how often a person who is about to be fired has no clue things are as bad as they are—because often the managers and the people around them have hidden from them how serious their suckage is. Nobody talks to them about it; the rest of the staff just becomes cold and less inclusive, which puts the perpetrator on the defensive, which digs the hole deeper. (Donna used to keep a sign in her office as a reminder to managers. It read, HAVE YOU HAD A CON-VERSATION TODAY? The idea was to remind bosses to talk to staffers they were having a problem with *before* coming to her, in her role as HR leader. Donna, like any normal person, did not relish the managers coming to her office announcing that they were ready to fire an employee when they had not even tried to find out why the employee was unable or unwilling to perform.)

Well, it's exactly the same in your personal life. Believe it or not, your partner is not in the relationship to consciously screw it up—though he may be doing just that.

Helping him on his personal self-improvement journey means approaching him with the basic precept that he means well. If you've been disappointed in the past, this may be extremely difficult. We understand; we've been there. Putting yourself in his shoes first, and knowing that your point of view on the relationship is not the *only* point of view, may be a first step toward healing. When we say "put yourself in his shoes" we do not mean, "Make excuses for him." (You've probably been doing that already—that's what got you to read this book.) But understanding your husband's intentions, if not his actions, can help modulate your anger.

Think of this—as we call it in business—as *relationship management*.

Two people who come at a problem with only their self-interest hardly ever end up solving the problem. But if these people acknowledge they have a shared goal, and do that by figuring out what makes the other person tick, the chances for success and resolution are far greater.

Relationship management comes down to this: *If I can figure out how you're wired, we can both get what we want.*

Show Him How to Set Goals: Or rather, show him how *you* set goals, and hope he will follow your example. If someone is unhappy, it is easy to focus on the roadblocks to a goal rather than on the goal itself. Essentially, goal setting in business happens in five stages:

1. Clarify your values: What's important to you, and what isn't?

2. Set priorities: What needs to happen when?

3. Set a challenging but achievable goal: You always want to challenge yourself—to shoot for Plan A, not immediately settle for Plan B. But at the same time, the goal has to be within the realms of rationality. Donna might want to be a professional basketball player, but it's not going to happen. Julie wants to become a country music singer, which is a wonderful goal, except for her complete and utter inability to carry a tune. Similarly, while we wanted our husbands to Think Big, we wanted them to still have some goals they could realistically achieve without, saying, growing seven inches or developing the world's fastest left arm. Being a cop was, for Phillip, a realistic goal, but still one that challenged him, mentally and physically.

4. Develop an action plan: If the goal meant more school, more training, more networking—whatever. The idea is to break down a goal into logical steps, and go forth in the right direction.

   For example, Phillip decided he wanted to be a cop. That required certain steps. He had to fill out the application, had to start doing regular workouts so he could pass the physical fitness portion of the test, had to pass psychological evaluations, etc. So he had to think through what steps/tasks would be required and go from there. These were all things that were out of Julie's control. She couldn't, for example, take the test for him or force him to go on a four-mile run each day; he had to do these things for himself. And of course, in the end, the success or failure—in this case, the success—was his, and his alone.

5. Build in incentives to keep you motivated: An incentive might be something as large as "Buy a new house when we've saved $50,000 dollars" or "Buy an ice cream when I've made that call I've been dreading all week." There are a thousand incentives to fit every occasion.

Ask Yourself: Does He Learn and Process Information Entirely Differently from Me? In HR, we use a personality test called the Myers-Briggs, which measures people in four areas, subdivided by two functions:

- How a person relates to others (either by Extraversion or Introversion)
- How a person takes in information (either by Sensing or Intuition)
- How a person makes decisions (either by Thinking or Feeling)
- How a person orders his or her life (either by Judging or Perceiving)

Here are a few typical Myers-Briggs questions. (If you're interested, there are many Web sites, like www.humanmetrics.com, which allow you to administer some adaptation of the test.)

1. As a rule, current preoccupations worry you more than your future plans.
2. You find it difficult to talk about your feelings.
3. You feel at ease in a crowd.
4. You do your best to complete a task on time.
5. You are strongly touched by stories about people's troubles.
6. You are more interested in a general idea than in the details of its realization.
7. Strict observance of the established rules is likely to prevent a good outcome.
8. Often you prefer to read a book than go to a party.
9. You tend to rely on your experience rather than on theoretical alternatives.
10. It's difficult to get you excited.

At the end of a long series of questions, you are rated according to your degree of introversion or extraversion, your tendency to process information based on your intellect or your intuition; your way of arriving at decisions (influenced more by thinking or feeling), and whether you order your life based on internal judgments or based more on external observation/perception of what's going on. Managers use the test to determine if a person is in the right kind of job, with the right kind of responsibilities—and if there are any strong personality conflicts within a department, whether those conflicts may be solved with a slight rejiggering of personnel, based on their personality features.

We're not saying you should administer the test to your partner (or reassign him to another woman!). But we are suggesting that you consider the ways he may be learning and processing information, which may be radically different from your own. Let's say the two of you are hunting for a house. If, for example, you are like Julie—a person who approaches a task intellectually (gathering as much information from other sources as she can, analyzing the problem, making judgments based on whatever facts she's gathered), and your husband is an extrovert like Phillip who's much more likely to act from the gut (going with his feelings, making judgments based not on "book learning" but perhaps from his intuitive sense of what would be right) . . . well, right there you've got a possibility for conflict. You will want to research the price value of properties in the surrounding area, check the rating of the local school system, look into the water table and the property taxes and the last time the roof was repaired. He will walk in, see the airiness and light and smell the coffee the realtor has cleverly brewed, and come away with a feeling from the place: *This is where we should live.*

But understanding your partner's approach at least helps you know that there are many valid ways for different personalities to approach a problem, and while the two of you may not have the same process or even the exact same solution, you may both end up with solutions that work—that is, it might take longer, but you can eventually find a house with a solid roof, an excellent school system, AND the right atmosphere!

Consider His Medical Status: As we've said before, many men are not the best conservators of their own health. And as they start reevaluating their lives, they may look at mental and financial issues but readily gloss over how medical difficulties are taking a toll on them. Memory loss, chronic pain, limited mobility, hearing loss, circulation problems that impede sexual performance . . . a host of health conditions can affect a relationship.

Sometimes solutions are straightforward—a hearing aid, for instance, or a prescription for Viagra. Sometimes, more far-reaching solutions are needed.

It took a long time for Phillip to admit his "casual" drinking was having more than a casual effect on his health: He had gained a lot of weight and was generally unmotivated. No amount of nagging on Julie's part made the slightest difference. The only thing that made a difference was an ultimatum: Beer or me.

Once Phillip moved out and landed his dream job, he realized he had chosen beer over his family. It was a pretty lonely existence, and he was left with the choice to only have beer, or to have everything else. That was when he began to exercise and stopped drinking. While Julie couldn't have stopped him from drinking, she could be a companion to him in sobriety—so though alcohol had never been a major problem for her, she stopped drinking just to keep Phillip company. Encouraged by her support, a forty-pound weight loss, and the return of his energy, he stopped smoking, too (with a little help from a nicotine patch). Phillip is still learning how to have fun without booze, but it definitely helps to have a wife who can have fun along with him.

Accept That There Are Some Aspects of His Personality That Will Never, Ever, Ever Evolve: *The Three Stooges:* Excruciating to watch, aren't they? Grown men punching one another in the face and falling down and going woo-woo-woo. And yet the man you love, the father of your children, the man who you get naked with, thinks they are brilliant. Makes you kind of queasy to contemplate, right? And yet: You must come to terms with it. You must reconcile yourself, once and for all, to his firm conviction that Bill O'Reilly is a man of the people or baby-chick yellow is an acceptable color for a grown man to wear or that going to a basketball game is more important than the Gucci sample sale. You must embrace the annoying things about him that, if you think about them too long, make you want to saw off your own head.

For Donna, that annoyance is Dave's chronic lateness. Years of nagging and whining later, she has not made the slightest difference in his ability to get from point A to point B with any punctuality. Finally, when she thought about this problem within the context of being the master of her own discontent, Donna realized he was never going to change because he didn't care about being late and there was no way she would ever succeed in making him care. Ultimately, she found the solution by doing something she always considered beneath her: lying. She tells Dave they have to be at any given place thirty minutes before they actually have to be there. She keeps it a secret from everyone, including her children. (Now, if he reads this, the gig is up.)

Let Go of the Fantasy That You Are the Source of All Joy: If men have received the cultural message that change is for wussies, women have received an equally destructive one: that if a man does not want to change himself, we can do it for him—that, in essence, we are capable of making him happy.

It's true that all of us can do a lot to add to someone else's misery index if we're cruel, thoughtless, and neglectful. But to create happiness and personal satisfaction for someone else is an impossible task—albeit one to which many women devote themselves. So it's critical that the men in our lives work to find their own equanimity, their own satisfaction with themselves, apart from us and our caretaking. That is part of every individual's evolution.

This became one of the biggest challenges for Dave. Donna kept telling him that if he focused on himself, did what he needed to do to make himself happy, the rest would come. After years of trying, Donna acknowledged she was not capable of or responsible for making him happy, and his unhappiness was not her fault.

But after Dave moved out, he became more focused than ever on the idea that he and Donna should get back together. It became his goal. The "good" Dave is the one who accomplishes the goals he sets—he's as determined as a pit bull; the bad Dave is more of a basset hound: *Hello, let me loll on the sofa and shed on your furniture.* He eventually wanted Donna to go into couples counseling with him when for years Donna had been begging him to do just that, and he refused. Now that it was his idea, it was imperative they go RIGHT NOW. The man who had for years insisted that counseling was a waste of time, that anyone who went to a counselor might as well just get a divorce, was now looking at counseling as his possible salvation.

Donna told Dave she would go if he found the therapist, made the appointment, scheduled the babysitter, paid for the sitter, and picked her up for the appointment(s). Since Donna thought this was about as likely as tax breaks for the middle class, she assumed she'd bought herself some time—because in truth, at this point Donna didn't want to go. She thought it was a waste of time and energy, since she'd already determined they wouldn't be getting back together. But she softened when Dave pointed out to her that whatever their future as a couple, they were connected forever as parents—and needed to learn to cooperate on that level.

The "good Dave," the man Donna had fallen in love with, made all the arrangements. About ten days later he called to let her know he would be picking her up for the appointment at seven PM the following week. Donna was startled, a little annoyed—and also, perhaps, hopeful.

Lose Your Fear of Therapy: For months, Donna and Dave were in marriage counseling; Donna went with Dave every two weeks, and Dave went by himself weekly. Donna had been in and out of therapy since she was twenty-two, so she felt she already had a fairly good idea of her "baggage"—what was fixable, what wasn't, how her tendency to be controlling could trip her up. But she hadn't looked at herself too carefully in the context of the marriage. And Dave—who came from a poor and emotionally troubled household—hadn't looked at himself *at all.* He knew he didn't want to recreate the home life he'd had; but he simply didn't have the tools to know how to create something different.

Counseling isn't for everyone—but if the going gets tough, everyone should at least consider seeking help, if not with a psychologist, then through community resources, your family doctor, or at your place of worship. (The Web site for the American Association for Marriage and Family Therapy [http://www.aamft.org] provides information on how to choose a marriage therapist.) For counseling to work, we learned it takes two things: the desire for both partners to evolve individually *and* as partners in a marriage.

For Donna and Dave, counseling was key. The most important strategy the therapist gave Donna was teaching her not to become mired in grudges and habits of the past. Donna needed to stop trying to recreate the beginning of her marriage and get to a place where she was starting something new with Dave for the right reasons. This was her breakthrough because, up until then, Donna could not drag herself out of the past to recognize the progress Dave had made and the commitment to change that he had already started implementing.

Donna also had to own up to the fact that many of the problems in communication, which she'd always blamed on Dave, were also hers. When he did not respond to her after years of begging and cajoling, she shut down. Part of her therapy was to learn to talk to her husband again. For years, she interpreted his stony silence as a form of rejection, perhaps even of contempt. She had to take the risk that talking to him again would be worth it.

Our men had to make two kinds of changes. Some changes were made for us. (For Julie, not drinking was the deal breaker for the whole relationship.) Other changes were for themselves. (Phillip wanted to hone his identity, and he ended up defining himself as a police officer, a hobby photographer—and a nonsmoker.) But in truth, *all* the changes were done for themselves, because these changes made their lives workable again.

CHAPTER 10

Epilogue

Where We Are Today—and What Our Husbands Have to Say

• • • • •

> Change is the law of life and those
> who look only to the past or present
> are certain to miss the future.
>
> —JOHN F. KENNEDY

Have you heard of the Hawthorne Effect? In the late nineteen twenties and early nineteen thirties, Harvard Business School professor Elton Mayo conducted a series of experiments on factory workers at the Hawthorne Plant of the Western Electric Company in Cicero, Illinois. The idea was to change certain factors in the workplace to see which changes increased productivity. The researchers started out by examining the physical and environmental influences of the workplace (such as brightness of lights, humidity) and later, moved into the psychological aspects (for instance breaks, group pressure, working hours, managerial leadership). Mayo found something very interesting: It almost didn't matter what kind of change was implemented.

Change, in and of itself, increased productivity, because workers felt they were being asked for their input in the workplace; they were receiving attention; their voices were heard. The study was seminal in helping management understand the importance of social dynamics of groups in the workplace. Employees who believe that changes are being made to respond to their needs—regardless of what those changes are—will improve performance.

Now in business, that doesn't mean that endless tinkering with the workplace, product, or staff is invariably a good thing: Too much change telegraphs indecision and incompetence. (*"Don't these people know what they're doing?"*) But change that seems to be for the common good says, "We are responsive to your needs."

Our point here is simple: Change that seems to be borne of the desire to improve your marriage is likely to *genuinely* improve your marriage. And oddly, even change that doesn't work out as planned may bring improvements—because you are actively working to make the marriage whole again, and your mate will be grateful you're trying to address his needs.

Each of us watched our marriage dissolve over the course of several years—then took about a year to get the marriage back on track. Our problems were global; we hope yours aren't. But what happened, through the subtle process of engagement and disengagement that is the Scorecard, was a rebirth of our love as our husbands became reinvested in their lives. They became participants in family life again *for themselves,* not because we were nagging them. They wanted and needed us, but as men, not as children—they learned they could stand on their own two feet.

And strangely, we brought about these changes by becoming

less like the entitled, critical, nagging, angry people we were at home—ruled by our emotions and neediness—and more like the people we were at work: positive, direct, honest (but diplomatic), polite, and considerate. Our work selves were not our phony personas; our work selves were, in fact, the best of us. Even when we are not at work, we experience this. Think of the last time you went to a convenience store, stopped by the library, bought groceries—how did you treat complete strangers? Treat your family better than you treat the checkout person at your local grocer. Always.

First, of course, there were the concrete, everyday changes. We delineated household duties based on our mutual strengths and weaknesses instead of on outmoded gender roles that determined what we thought our husbands "should" and "shouldn't" do. According to Julie, Phillip has channeled his energy and compulsivity into housework. Now, by comparison *she's* the slob. And Phillip has become so competent at doing things like calling our service providers that often he reminds Julie to pay bills before they're actually due. (Julie says, "Mental note to self: Be careful what you wish for.")

Donna is also grateful for the partnership she and Dave have formed. Things at home run much more smoothly, and there are real discussions to plan an approach to handle situations that arise. While party planning used to be much more in Donna's realm, Dave is now making plans of his own. This fall, Dave decided to have an Oktoberfest and planned the entire event—every last knockwurst, beer, and polka. Donna asked how she could help, but Dave took the lead and Donna worked from a list of errands and shopping items.

In general: Laundry is folded, dishes are washed, bills are paid. All of these things may not happen *exactly* the way we want. But there is no more arguing about the way to get to the destination. Take the highway, take the scenic route, we don't care: JUST GET THERE AND WE'RE HAPPY.

Our sexual and romantic lives have changed, too. Of course, if you asked us and our husbands why they've changed, we'd probably have different answers: They might say our domestic lives have changed because we have sex more, and we would say we have sex more because our domestic lives have changed. Both of us have had to redefine, to some extent, our ideas of intimacy. Julie came home one day recently, thoroughly exhausted; in the past, the fight would have been about her fatigue, about how she never made time for sex. Now, Phillip knows that it is as important to her agenda as his, even if not *right this minute*; just knowing she wants him, in the general sense, makes a difference. Phillip got a blanket and they sat together, holding hands and watching football. The football game, of course, was Julie's part of the compromise—but she realized that when love returns, even watching football with your husband can be romantic!

As much as we love to talk about the change in our husbands—which is real and substantive—we've had to change as much as they have. We're not just better wives but better mothers, friends, and sisters as well. We've had to be both tougher *and* softer, depending on the occasion. Tougher in not stepping in to clean up every mess; softer in the sense of redefining what *we* think of as mess—which may, in fact, be another approach. And sometimes a better one. As Donna explains:

I have a much tighter rein on myself. If I'm going to delegate, I can't be angry if a project doesn't come out exactly the way I envisioned it. I really do believe I'm the most wonderful creature on this planet, and I have to allow myself to recognize that just because Dave brings a different approach to many things, it's not of less value.

Julie, too, has worked hard to manage her expectations and appreciate small victories:

It's embarrassing to admit, but I had a huge problem with entitlement. I think I was so used to Phillip not doing anything, that when he finally started to turn his life around I wanted to say, "You should have been doing this three years ago!" instead of "Thank you, I appreciate it." I still have problems in this arena, showing my gratitude, but it's something I'm commited to working on.

Of course, our relationships are not perfect, and there's much that has not changed—and accepting that fact has been part of our journey, too. In the land of trivia, Julie will not relinquish doing her beloved taxes, and Phillip will continue to insist he does not need receipts, because he can keep all the figures in his head. (This, from a man who in ten years still cannot remember that Julie's favorite kind of chocolate is not See's or Godiva but the cheap stuff from the drugstore.) More important, Phillip is trying to figure out his next career step—because now he *has* a career. And Julie is trying to figure that out as well. But this time, because of his steady paycheck and new-found attitude toward work, she may get to be the one to pursue her dreams—maybe going back to school, getting another degree, or opening a small shop in the neighborhood. It is an ongoing conversation, and one not loaded with tension.

Donna will probably never balance her checkbook and hates paying bills, so they leverage Dave's attention to detail—and she smiles when she opens the desk drawer and sees his color-coordinated files. And Dave's utilization of his detail skills has opened his eyes to the many, many expenses that managing a household requires. This, in turn, helps to balance Dave's choices on discretionary items. He now has a much clearer sense of what's being spent and when expenses happen.

We think it's only fair that after talking for hundreds of pages about ourselves and our marriages, our husbands should get the last word. How did *they* feel about the Scorecard—about how it changed them, and us? We'll shut up now, and let them speak for themselves.

DAVE

You know what put me on the path to change? The realization that I was lonely. Lonely in my own home, in my own marriage. Because I had shut down so completely. Partially, I'd shut down because I was disappointed and angry—at Donna, and at myself.

First of all, I never saw my wife. She was coming home at seven, eight PM. We had no intimate life—life was just a series of chores, with no real communication between us. I had thought being a stay-at-home father would be fun—and for a little while it was. But I think only certain guys can have a good sense of themselves and be stay-at-home fathers . . . and I wasn't one of them.

So I was bored, I had no companionship, and I think I sort of gave up. I started drinking more. I was going out and coming home at four in the morning. I told myself I was still the same person I'd always been—that, for example, I was still a generous person. But it's easy to be generous with someone else's money. I was spending the money Donna earned going out entertaining myself and friends. At first Donna didn't even notice, because she was working so hard— and she went to sleep early. This saddened me, too. When she did realize I was out all night, she was so angry, and I was so angry and . . . well, we had backed ourselves into our separate lonely corners and couldn't talk about it.

Drinking numbed everything; it allowed me to coast. And I think it was the way I medicated my underlying depression—not very smart, considering that alcohol is a depressant. But it's something many, many guys do. I became a semi-interested, barely functioning observer of my own life.

But gradually, I began to become more and more frightened. I had been frightened before I left the house and became even more frightened after. I was seeing a woman who wasn't even my type. She was a drinking companion, and she listened to me. But I realized I was going to lose everything that was important to me. The worst part was thinking about what my absence would do to my children. Coming from a difficult family background, I knew the harm it would cause. I've known lots of guys and women who've left for good; nothing good ever comes of it.

Things began to turn around when I got a job: I knew I couldn't continue to go out every night and still function. So I had to stop. Drinking was an escape that prevented me from fully participating in my own life, from being in a family. But besides that, it took me a long time to realize I needed to talk—to a therapist, and to Donna.

Like a lot of guys I grew up believing that if you had a problem, you dealt with it yourself. I didn't know how to share it. You can't be part of a family with that attitude.

I really do think I've changed, and counseling has helped. At first everything was about me, about what I could do to make myself happy, not what I can do to make the family happy. I had to get my priorities straight, and I had to realize that when an issue comes up, I can't put it off—because for me, putting stuff off means it'll never get done. I still struggle with this a lot.

It wasn't just me who had to go to counseling, though; we needed to go together, so I could say, without fear of being criticized, what was bothering me. Donna has learned how to be less critical—and how important praise is to me. Maybe I wasn't getting enough before. And while she's certainly a very talkative person, I wasn't getting the kind of talk that I valued.

Now, we talk to each other every night, right after the kids go to bed. It doesn't have to be a long conversation; it usually isn't. But still, we talk about our day, about anything new that's happened; we really make a point of sharing with each other. At first that might seem kind of forced, but eventually it becomes second nature. It's certainly an improvement over how we used to communicate. Some days, all we said was "Hi" and " 'Bye." And it sounds strange, coming from a guy who isn't good at talking . . . but because I wasn't good at putting my thoughts into words, which I am still working to improve, I actually need to talk more than some people because I need the practice.

You know how kids look on Christmas morning when they get something very, very special . . . the train set or the bike or the puppy? There's delight, and a little bit of fear: Is this really mine? Will this great thing be taken away from me?

That's the look my kids had when we told them I'd be moving back into the house. I'll always remember that look. It still can bring tears to my eyes.

PHILLIP

It's not like I didn't know this to begin with: Julie and the kids are my most prized possessions. They've ALWAYS been the most important thing to me. But I was so depressed about my own life, I was in a state of denial about everything. Including their importance in my life.

I was always working, always had a job. But I felt . . . not complete. Insufficient. I wasn't doing anything productive. I had been in the military, and I was proud of that. And after that, it was one crappy job after another. And there was Julie, climbing the corporate ladder, and it felt like I was just . . . on my belly, crawling. Crawling away from my family, away from myself.

Strangely enough, getting accepted to the police academy coincided with being kicked out of the house. So just as I was getting on the right track professionally, my home life was in shambles. By that point, Julie had had enough of my empty promises about what I was going to do with my life; she wanted me to get it together on my own, without her help. The first night I spent without my wife or kids or dogs was probably the most depressing night of my life.

I admit now that I probably needed to get kicked out of the house. I'd gotten complacent and lazy and felt she'd always be there. And then when she wasn't, I was heartbroken, devastated. She'd kicked me out and moved on with her life.

But while she was pushing me away, I pushed back. I kept telling her I was going to change—and showing her. At first, she was so resistant that we never talked more than a sentence or two. All our conversations were not much more than, "When are you picking up the kids?" or—worse—"How long will you be here and when are you leaving?" But I was persistent.

I worked really hard to regain her trust. I was like Hercules performing the twelve labors—and truly, I would have slain every lion and cleaned every stable to make her love me again. I still remember the feeling I had when Julie agreed, once again, to hold my hand. It was as great as the first night we spent together.

There will always be some things that drive the other person crazy. She still can't stand my inattention to financial details. (Though I would like to say, for the record, that I've never bounced a check . . . ask Julie how many she's bounced!) And when I get home, that's it; I can put my job behind me. She can't. I also have to deal with her working late, which has always been something we argued about. I've found that if I cook something she really likes, she gets home much faster. Now, in fact, I take care of almost everything around the house, and she sometimes complains about how long I take to, say, do the lawn. Not much of a complaint, right?

When I was drinking, everything became a vicious cycle: Feeling unloved, I'd drink more; drinking more, I became someone you wouldn't want to be around. These days are very different. I do feel the love—though sometimes it may take the form of worry. Usually, Julie doesn't fret too much about my being a beat cop. But every now and then I'll walk out the door without saying good-bye, or kissing the kids, and she'll come running after me and say, "What if something happened to you today?" And I stop, and come back, and kiss the kids, and kiss her. We try to remember, every day, what's truly important.

The Christmas of the year Donna and Dave got back together, Dave asked his wife what she wanted for the holidays. Instead of making him guess, as she might have in the past, she gave him a list of twenty-five items to choose from, assuming he'd pick one or two. He went out and got all twenty-five. (Overspending: still a little issue between them. Donna repeated to herself, like a mantra: Just be happy. And hope he ran into a few good sales.)

On the evening Julie and Phillip finally got back together, Julie donned a tiny little outfit she'd bought for the occasion, and sparks flew; one of those sparks turned out to be their third child, Hunter, born about nine months later. More recently, in October 2005, they sealed the deal with their fourth child, Olivia Grace—an apt name, considering Julie does feel, in some sense, that she lives in a state of grace she never dreamed of before.

Phillip and Julie got new wedding bands and put away their old ones.

The new ones had a similar style—but they sparkled.

Acknowledgments

If you had told us three years ago that almost getting divorced would be one of the best things that ever happened to us or that we'd be writing a book about it, we'd have thought you the most insensitive of opportunists. This was the most heartbreaking time of our lives. Funny how life changes.

We thought, in our darkest hours, that the best we could hope for would be an eventual sense of empowerment because we had learned to live our own lives and had become successful single parents. How sad and defeatist this now sounds.

While the need to face the facts and be pragmatic is part of who we both are, what we've also learned to believe is that we really do create our own reality and influence our own destiny. We can make our dreams come true. We came to understand that love can be rekindled and fires once dead can build to even greater heat.

How do you tell a good friend that she's crazy? That you love her and appreciate her confidence, but who has the time to write a book with kids, jobs, husbands, and other commitments? And even if we found the time, we weren't writers (except in our dreams!). To Candy Lee, our muse and catalyst. The ultimate networker, deal-doer, empowerer, and role model! Thank you so very, very much.

With gratitude . . .

To Reiter-man, our agent extraordinaire. Who, after golf and cocktails in the beautiful Virgin Islands, fell in love with our story and captained us on this incredible journey.

And Judith. Incredible, warm, funny, so-very-talented Judith. After trial and error, we finally found our soul sister who "got us" and our senses of humor (of utmost importance). Who seemed to know exactly where we were coming from and helped us bring our story to life in an unexpected and delightful way— even if she didn't believe that people could change (we think we've convinced her otherwise!).

To our families, who didn't blink an eye when we told them we were going to write a book and who have been endless sources of support and encouragement as we've balanced the writing of our story with many competing demands—the surest evidence of healthy partnerships. Philip and Chelsea and Lauren, Madelyn, Hunter, and baby Olivia—you are our greatest joys and the magnets that keep us together. We adore you.

Dad, Mom, Karyn, Justin, and the rest of my family—thank you for helping me become who I am today. God knows that helping me build character wasn't easy, I love you all. Phil, Cherie, Noelle, CL & Co, and the rest of the Voorhees—thank you for welcoming me into your family . . . if I could have picked any family in the world to be part of—I still would have picked yours.

Meeg—your friendship keeps me grounded—thank you for everything. Julie

To our friends who walked with us through some of our darkest days, allowing us to cry on your shoulders no matter what time of day or night. There is a quote—"friends are the family you choose." We chose well.

And to you, our reader, who will get to know us a little by reading our story. We hope you enjoy the book and, most important, find it useful in helping you solve your relationship problems, be they big or small. We so appreciate you.

P.S. We still cry, we still argue, we sometimes sink exhausted in defeat. But now, we also see a path where there once was a closed door, and we know there are ways forward and ways back.

God, thank you for proving once again that everything happens for a reason.

Appendix

Your One-Year Scorecard

....

Here is a chance to chart your progress over the course of a year. On the horizontal axis is the year, marked off by months; on the vertical axis we'd like you to note each item in the area of the marriage you're working on. We have provided one sample chart, but we encourage you to keep track of your progress in the areas most important to you.

Communicate: Become My Friend	Talk about what you're thinking and feeling	Share your opinions and preferences	Speak your mind in an honest and constructive way	Open up about what's bothering you	Don't Yell!!!!
I/N					
S/D					
January	Keeping up with nightly 15-minute talk of what's going on before bedtime	Solicited opinions on house renovation; listened; did not have huge fight	10-year anniversary. Celebrated with sex, long talk	Instead of clamming up, Husband has discussed something that's been weighing on his mind for three months. Progress!	TOO MUCH YELLING
February					
March					
April					

SAMPLE

Communicate: Become My Friend	Keep me apprised of what's going on in your life	Don't make unilateral decisions	Remember that we have a partnership	Show interest in my work and my life as an individual	Don't take out your anger about other problems on me
I/N					
S/D					
January	Keeping up with nightly 15-minute talk of what's going on before bedtime	Husband sank $3,000 into an entertainment center without discussing with me; need to work on not making unilateral decisions.	Less yelling; have cleared the air about holiday disagreement	Husband asked me about my work twice this week; actually seemed to listen	Shouting down from 3 times a week in March to once a week now
February					
March					
April					

SAMPLE

	I/N	S/D	January	February	March	April

May	June	July	August	September	October	November	December

About the Authors

....

Julie Bell is director of Strategic Sourcing at United Airlines and holds an M.B.A. from Rider University. She lives in Chicago with her husband and their four extraordinary children.

Donna Brown is director of Corporate Human Resources for United Airlines, and lives in a suburb of Chicago with her hero-husband, Dave, and their two wonderful children.